Beat Route

Jools Holland

Beat Route

First published in Great Britain 1998
by Victor Gollancz
An imprint of the Cassell Group
Wellington House, 125 Strand, London WC2R 0BB

Beat Route is an NVC ARTS and Initial production for BBC and NPS

Beat Route – based on an original concept by NVC ARTS

A catalogue record for this book is available
from the British Library.

ISBN 0 575 06700 4

Designed and set by Production Line, Minster Lovell, Oxford
Printed in Great Britain by Butler & Tanner Ltd, Frome, Somerset

98 99 5 4 3 2 1

Contents

Credits

First of all I would like to thank my co-author, Harriet Vyner, for patiently asking pertinent questions and then maintaining a permanent look of being incredibly interested in the answers; and Geoff Wonfor for being himself at all times – that self being one of the greatest directors that the world of film and television has ever known – and one of the dearest friends a person could wish for. I would like to thank all the people involved in the production of *Beat Route*: Rocky Oldham and Malcolm Gerrie at Initial Films; Ceetah Grieves, Lizzie Pole, James Wills at NVC; Henk van der Meulen at NPS; Mark Thompson, Nicola Gooch, Nicola Hill and Jane Root at the BBC. All the people on the crew: Sara Brailsford, Nick Samwell-Smith, Sally Westbury, Eugene O'Connor, Carol Woof, Dave Hayes, Andy Matthews, Tim Fraser, Kate Fenhalls, Ali Hendessi and Peter Row. All the artists, performers and members of the public who have taken part. My agent, Paul Loasby; Humphrey Price at Victor Gollancz; Julian Alexander at LAW. And especially to Valerie McCartney for helping to make this happen.

Jools Holland

Introduction

My first experience of travelling wasn't very pleasant: I'd never been abroad before and didn't know what to expect. Squeeze were on tour in Holland, and we were in a Luton box Transit van; there were no windows, it *was* just a box. You could sit in the bit above the cab, though, where there was a small hole, about one inch across, which we took turns to look out of.

Not one of us had ever been abroad before – we were all sixteen, seventeen, eighteen years old – so we were rather excited. However, all I can remember now is the intense cold. If you think of those Old Master paintings of lots of people skating round, that's what it looked like. Fortunately – and I was the only one to be this lucky – I had a fur coat with me, and it probably saved my life.

So, when preparing for a journey, one of the first things to do is try to find out what the weather is going to be like. On my first trip to America, for instance, in the summer of 1978, Squeeze drove in un-air-conditioned vehicles through the boiling-hot southern states, and I'd brought a fur coat and snowboots (which I had for my motor bike). This was only the second time I'd been abroad, and I'd imagined it was always going to be as cold as Holland. This time I nearly roasted to death.

Also I had all this stuff that I was carrying around with me, so another tip I can pass on is: don't buy lots of big things near the beginning of your trip. I had a huge tin lorry that I'd bought for my young brother, and a gigantic kit of a hot-rod which I had to carry everywhere.

What articles *do* I carry on my trips? A guidebook's handy, and a sketchbook (I find photographs too unreliable). A compass, curiously enough, isn't such a bad thing, although it's made a mockery of these days. And a diary. What else do I have in my bag? Pencils. Tickets, of course, and foreign currency. Amusements, as magazines can get boring. A talking dictionary is better than a magazine.

The other thing is to bring your own sandwiches, because the food on planes, even in first class, isn't particularly great. In fact nine times out of ten it's really terrible. If you take your sandwiches you won't be disappointed. I'd recommend a few thick ones on crusty farmhouse bread, maybe cheese and piccalilli, roast beef and horseradish, things you might not find abroad.

On that first trip to Holland, as I shivered and peered through the tiny hole, one of the first things that struck me was the sight of people driving on the other side of the road. It is quite easy to learn to drive on the wrong side of the road, which a lot of the world does, but it's not so easy to learn how to *cross* the road. This is because it's been drummed into you since you were a very small child to look a certain way when you cross the road. So you check into your hotel and you think, Right, I'm going off into the streets to get a flavour of the country I'm in. Nothing would spoil it more than stepping out and immediately being run over by a bus, or knocked down by a passing Fiat or Zil (they're what Russian presidents drive and look very similar to Cadillacs. The only car manufacturer that begins with Z that I know of). Everything else you can become acclimatized to, but just drop your guard for a moment, step into the road and look left instead of right and *bang* – it could all be over.

Another thing is to try to insist on a hotel room with a view. Some people say, 'Oh, you do make a fuss,' but if I go to a hotel that hasn't got much of a view and I'm going to be there for a few days, then I do everything possible to change it. Because the whole point of going somewhere abroad is that you want to see what's going on.

Now a few tips about airports. One of the most boring things about airports is the time it can take to get from the terminal to the plane. So the smaller the airport the better. At the big airports like Heathrow there are so many terminals it's easy to get lost, and if you get to the wrong one you could miss your flight as it could take you an hour to get from one terminal to another. If, however, you're lucky enough to be travelling from somewhere like London City Airport or Antwerp, there is only one small building, where the same bloke collects your ticket and searches you and everything.

The other thing is, you don't want to waste time being stopped by customs. Try not to limp, as they have a policy of always stopping people with limps. This is because they assume they've got things concealed in their shoes. As a rule it's best to try to blend in as much as possible, as they are always looking out for the suspicious or unusual. I realized this when I was wearing a very well-cut (I thought) suit, which I had just had a tailor make for me. Going through customs, I was pulled to one side and they went through everything. I said afterwards, 'Out of interest, why did you stop me?' 'It was your baggy ill-fitting suit, it might have concealed something.' So I was not only delayed but also insulted.

In Cancun Airport they just have a button at customs. You present yourself in front of these traffic lights and you press the button when it is your turn to go through. If it is green you go through, and if it's red you're stopped and searched. It doesn't matter if you're the Archbishop of Canterbury; if it's red you're searched and that's it. If the light's green, you could be a well-known drug dealer with a huge double-sided suitcase, great belts full of heroin or something, and they'd wave you straight through. It's just a gamble.

And here's another thing: always make sure you have your passport. I *have* travelled without a passport and you *can* get by. You're put in a room with what are described as 'undesirable aliens', and questioned. It is really inconvenient, especially when the band's waiting.

I was deeply offended when I first went to Australia, because men would come on the plane with masks and spray the cabin with disinfectant – while you're sitting right there – which I always took rather personally. There used to be a particular flight to Australia on which people regularly died. They were often elderly, and they'd be seeing their relatives for the last time, so in spite of their will to live the excitement was just too much. We asked about this when Squeeze travelled to Australia. They told us: 'Well, we would normally remove the person into first class, the body, that is.' It was a packed plane and we were in economy class for thirty-six hours. So we all acted dead in order to get upgraded, but sadly it didn't work. You had to have the full symptoms, which was difficult enough, but even if you did get upgraded, although you got the wider seat you didn't get all the nicer food. However, it's travelling in a band which really makes this type of thing enjoyable. It's not so much fun pretending to be dead on your own.

Of course, there are all sorts of stories of bands behaving wildly on aeroplanes. I remember once one of the band bought some dresses in America and on the way back he made the air hostess put one on and model it for him. She was the same sort of build as his wife, and he was impatient to see if it would suit her. Nowadays I can't imagine any airline allowing that. Years ago there were people going off for snogs and to smoke drugs in the toilets, but I think the crews are much better trained nowadays so they do that less often. (I expect my readers are wondering if I myself have ever been taken off into the toilet for a snog or whatever, but I am not prepared to divulge this information. That will have to wait for my next book.)

It is nice to purchase at least one souvenir from the country you've visited. After all, if you buy something for yourself and then get sick of it in a week, you can always give it to somebody else as a gift. They will be so grateful that you brought it all the way back for them.

However, you've got to be careful about the nature of the presents you buy, because even thoughtful gifts can be misunderstood by over-zealous customs officers. Take, for example, an early trip back from Amsterdam. I'd bought some vintage 1960s . . . I wouldn't say pornography, I'd say saucy photographs, saucy glamour stills, to give out as Christmas gifts. I explained this to the woman customs officer, who seemed to be looking at them with some distaste. With a scornful look, she flung them back at me with the words, 'Well, I'm glad I'm not getting any presents off you this year.'

Also, if you buy a souvenir, you have to make sure you can import it legally. On my first trip to Australia you could buy certain things in the airport shop which I'm sure you can't get any more. For instance, you could buy the stuffed head of a kangaroo. I think it's probably against the law now. It really is an interesting concept to get your national creature and stuff its head and flog it at the airport.

One final travelling tip: by and large buying things in the duty-free is no cheaper than anywhere else. Just go to the supermarket. In America it's still cheaper to buy a packet of cigarettes in the most expensive hotel than it is in the duty-free at Heathrow. I don't know why that is, but there you are.

What determined me to make this TV series was that Geoff Wonfer was going to do it with me. I first met Geoff in Newcastle when I went up to do *The Tube* in 1982, and we struck up an immediate friendship. He made two or three videos for me, and also did one for Squeeze. We have made several other films together, including one in New Orleans and others in Memphis, Nashville and Jamaica. Whenever I've been out filming with Geoff, it's been very enjoyable. You've got to enjoy what you're doing or there's no point in doing it. We were also reunited with Eugene O'Connor, the cameraman, whom we'd worked with before. So I knew we were going to have a good time.

Chicago

When I first learnt to play the piano, my uncle showed me the rudiments of boogie-woogie. I was only about eight years old, and desperate to get hold of any piano records. It was very hard, at that time, to get hold of boogie-woogie records. I didn't even know who made them.

But one day I went into the West End of London alone, which nowadays you'd think would not only be forbidden to an eight-year-old child, it would be illegal. But off I went to the West End, walking past the doorways of beckoning prostitutes and drug pushers, unaware of the sins of the world, skipping along in my baggy shorts. It would have been about 1966, we'd just won the World Cup and all was good in England. Where other children were happy to play on bombsites and discover hidden revolvers, or kick a tin can around, all that really wasn't for me. I simply loved playing the piano, so a lot of the time I was very happy to sit at home and just play.

I had been told that if I went to a shop called Dobells, I might get hold of a record that would help me to learn my favourite style of playing. So

I went in and there was a very helpful and benevolent assistant there, the sort one dreams of coming across in a record shop. He looked at me and could see I wasn't a big spender. 'Hello,' I said, 'I wonder if you could help me? I'm very interested in boogie-woogie piano and I've got enough to buy one record. What one should I get, do you think?' So he stacked up a big pile of records – there must have been at least ten of them – and said: 'There you are, young man, go into the booth and listen to those.' In those days they had a booth where you could listen to a track or two. I didn't know how this worked, never having been into this sort of shop before, so I played each record all the way through to the end. When I had got about halfway through the pile he tapped on the window and said, 'We close in a minute!' and I said, 'Oh well, I'd better come back tomorrow. I haven't finished listening to them yet. I've made a note of the ones I quite like, but I'm still not sure.' So I went back the following day and continued listening thoroughly, until finally I stumbled across this one record (I think it was a French import). It was called something like the *Kings of Boogie-Woogie*, and it had a rather unlikely sleeve. I've not seen anything like it since, and I've still got this record.

Boogie-woogie is quite a complex form of music to listen to, mainly because you're hearing a repetitive left-hand pattern with a fresh invention from the right hand. It is the contrast between these two patterns which gives the music its rhythm. In fact, it is based on the most ancient ideas of harmony, which feature in ancient Greek culture, for example. And I suspect that's why most people like the medium of the blues, as it is based on this classical form of harmony which everyone can respond to.

My record featured Jimmy Yancey, Albert Ammons, Pete Johnson and Meade Lux Lewis. Now I wasn't aware at that time that all these pianists came from Chicago, or that they had influenced people like Little Richard (who in turn influenced the Beatles and the Rolling Stones, who in turn influenced me). The thing that I *did* realize was that the music really thrilled me. I wanted to play the piano exactly like these people I was listening to, in the same way that I wanted to make a sound like the Beatles made. That is what excited me. I had no idea whether these people were living or dead. It was just another record, the same as a Beatles record.

So I took the record home and I would play it in my grandmother's front room in her terraced house in Greenwich. In the sixties, in these small terraced houses, it was traditional to have a piano in the front room. As soon as I had bought this one record, the only record I had, I spent ages listening to it and trying to copy it. The fact that I couldn't (quite) was probably just as well; I'd rather sound like me than someone else. But it had a very strong influence. Sometimes, when I got it right, it felt like the people on the record, Albert Ammons and Pete Johnson and Jimmy Yancey, were carrying on where my uncle had left off in teaching me about the piano. They were my spirit chums. So when it came to making this film in Chicago, I was particularly interested in finding out a little bit about them, and I wanted to go and lay flowers on both Albert Ammons' and Jimmy Yancey's graves.

The first time I visited Chicago was with Squeeze. All I knew about it was that it had the world's tallest building, the Sears Tower. I soon discovered it had a huge Polish community, because some Polish people befriended me, took me around and showed me some of the sights of the city. Then I realized what a divided place it was. There was a sort of line, which I had seen in cities before, but never quite as definitely as in Chicago. The black people lived in one part (the south side), the Polish community in another part and the Italian people in another, and people always seemed to stick to their own part of town.

Chicago was originally a trading post, where the Indians would trade all sorts of things with the white settlers. One of the goods was onions, and sometimes there was an onion mountain, like the butter mountain in Europe, and it started to stink. The indigenous American phrase for 'rotting onions' is *chi ca go*, and that's where Chicago gets its name from.

Boogie-woogie – a contrast of two patterns

However, it carried on being a trading post, and grew and grew in size because of its location on a great lake. Eventually it became this vast city, with several million inhabitants, all made of wood (the city that is, not the inhabitants). Of course it burnt down, in 1871. The cause of the fire was supposed to have been a woman milking her cow by candlelight; the cow moved and knocked the candle over and burnt the whole city down. This tale is a bit like the story of the Great Fire of London, which was supposed to have started in Pudding Lane, maybe by a baker leaving something in the oven too long. But of course nobody can ever be quite sure because all the evidence was burnt. The only building to survive the Chicago fire was a water tower, which was made of stone. Naturally, it has become a landmark. However, when Oscar Wilde visited the place he described it as looking like a 'castellated monstrosity covered in salt and pepper pots'.

Nowadays Chicago is a big industrial town which reminds me somewhat of Manchester or Liverpool. It has got huge stockyards where they trade in meat; and of course, most importantly, it has the blues clubs.

Geoff and I went to a place called the Chequerboard Lounge, which is one of the older blues clubs on the south side where people still play and listen to this music. There are still plenty of these clubs, as the people of Chicago realize the importance of the blues.

The next day we set off bright and early to explore some of the famous buildings in Chicago. The skyscrapers really are a marvel to look at as they follow the shoreline. First, there's the Sears Tower, which was once the tallest building in the world. There is also a rather fabulous psychiatric hospital which looks like a mad person designed it, and like it would drive you mad to be there.

Of course, Chicago is also famous for its Frank Lloyd Wright buildings. We were going to film in one of his buildings with Ramsey Lewis, the great Chicago pianist, but the only one I visited was possibly the most gloomy, unpleasant house I'd ever been in in all my life. Frank Lloyd Wright has a lot of fans but I'm not one of them. I'd rather live in a 1930s semi in Pinner than one of his houses. I do think he did some quite good industrial buildings, and I'd certainly champion those, but this house didn't have much humour, or wit, or even imagination come to that. It has a grand piano, but he so hated its unsymmetrical shape that he actually had it walled up. So there is just the keyboard of the piano showing, sticking out of the wall. This would have made it incredibly tricky to get into, for tuning and everything. A typical lack of imagination coupled with bullying tactics. But there were all these people traipsing around this house gasping at the marvel of it. I couldn't believe it. I wanted to shake them and say, 'But this is really *awful*.'

One of the many buildings that *did* appeal to me was the
Merchandise Mart. It is a huge 1930s building with many floors, full of
offices and shops and things like that. But on the front of it they have
these gigantic stone heads. The opera house in Budapest, I believe, has
the heads of great opera writers immortalized in stone. The Sheldonian
Theatre in Oxford has busts of the great Greek and Roman writers. And
here in Chicago the Merchandise Mart has chosen to immortalize the
great shopkeepers of the world in similar manner: Mr Woolworth, Mr
Sears, et cetera.

While we were filming, this official came along and kept saying we
weren't allowed to shoot the great shopkeepers' busts. Geoff took no
notice and just said, 'Carry on anyway,' down the walkie-talkie. It was
easy for him to say: he was over on the other side of the river, because
he'd wanted to film the scene from there. I was standing right next to this
angry bloke. I said rather urgently down the walkie-talkie: 'They are
telling us not to film here, Geoff, we had better move on.' Back down the
walkie-talkie (with the man standing next to me, able to hear every
word) came Geoff's piercingly loud voice: 'He's just a wanker, carry on
filming.' Thanks a lot, Geoff, big help.

Another famous landmark of Chicago is Bertrand Goldberg's Marina
City, completed in 1967. You can see from the photograph later in this
chapter why it's known as 'Corn Cob Towers'. They are ravishing 1960s
buildings, and they are used in *The Blues Brothers* for the car chase at the
end, which people might recognize them from.

Some of the skyscrapers really are a marvel. Apart from anything
else, how do they manage to stand up? Why don't they blow over? My
hotel was a skyscraper, so I could look out from my room on the 32nd
floor and marvel at the skyline. One night, as I looked out of my window,
I saw five or six spiders outside, battling with one another in the wind.
Imagine climbing up outside of the building, getting all that way and
having the energy to have a fight with the other spiders. Robert the Bruce
was inspired by watching his spider into thinking, I'm never going to

Chicago's fantastic skyline

give up, and I felt I'd learnt a lesson from this too. However, my lesson was rather different to Robert the Bruce's. It made me realize that in Chicago you can keep going up, but still never get anywhere at all. You just end up fighting with the other spiders. So there's no point in climbing and fighting; it's best just to sit down, relax, have a drink with everybody and not worry too much.

As I mention later, it is very important to make contact with taxi drivers when you're in a strange city. The first one we met here was nicknamed the Candyman, and he ran a dating agency from the confines of his taxi. It was rather charming. His own marriage had broken up, but he still ran a dating agency for the good of others, which was how he saw it. He kept this book in the back of his car, and you could look through and pick people you wanted to date. He told us he had succeeded in bringing two or three couples together, and he had even been invited to their weddings, which was rather nice. He also gave me sweets: the Candyman.

The taxi driver who picked us up outside Buddy Guy's Blues Club was less romantic. About seven of us had climbed in the taxi, all squashed in

together. This cab had a rather strange and pungent aroma to it. Then the driver offered to get us any girls we wanted; he said, 'Yeah, I can get you the girls.'

'But what would we do with them?'

'You can get them in the back of the car.'

'It's very kind of you, but we don't actually think they would fit,' we replied. It would have been physically impossible to get anybody else in. I was having to sit on Geoff's lap at the time as it was.

Chicago is the home not only of the blues, but also of the electric blues. This is where country blues and the New Orleans style of rhythm and blues blend, and the result sounds very different to both. A Chicago style evolved which used electric guitars in a more aggressive manner; this is related to British rhythm and blues. This is a musical tradition which I myself am part of. The Rolling Stones took the blues and turned it into their own thing and I take it from them.

So on our second day we visited Shirley Dixon, who is the great Willie Dixon's daughter. She runs the Blues Heaven Foundation, which helps get royalties for blues musicians and advises them generally. They've got a lot of archive footage of original recording sessions, and the whole foundation is supported by charitable donations, some of which come from the wealthier people in British music.

Willie Dixon is one of the greatest blues songwriters of all time. I played piano with him once in a show in New York, and he told me that blues songs are really concerned with telling a story, summing things up in a direct and truthful manner. He also said that it is a music for grown-ups and not for kids. The blues tends to be about things like infidelity, people hammering it too much, drinking too much or taking drugs, gossiping, or jealousy – not like pop music. Originally it would have been played to a crowd that would have both laughed and cried, and

The roof of the Candyman's cab – his dating agency

then probably had a big fight. I think that's why I've always been drawn to it. It has a serious story to tell.

Willie Dixon played the bass on all the Chuck Berry records. A lot of people think they know how to play Chuck Berry, but I suggest to them that they listen very carefully to 'Little Queenie', and its bass line. My bass player, Dave Swift, has transcribed it. It's so unusual that Dave told me that if he showed it to someone from a music school they would say, 'You're mad, you can't do this.' And Willy Dixon's a complete genius, because he played it, and it worked perfectly, and nobody else but him would have thought of doing it, or been *able* to do it.

Besides writing the great song 'Wang Dang Doodle', he also wrote 'I Just Wanna Make Love to You'. His version is real slow, and he sort of hollers: 'I just wanna make love to you.' He's not saying 'I love you' in a soppy teenage manner – this is the real thing.

The Blues Heaven Foundation is in the same building from where Marshall Chess ran the legendary Chess Records label. A lot of the famous Chess masterpieces were recorded here. Chuck Berry lived in the basement at one time; and when the Rolling Stones visited they were shocked to discover their hero Muddy Waters helping to redecorate the place, because he just had to find work doing anything he could.

Things have changed a lot from those days, and sometimes for the better. For example, Shirley told me that when her father used to go to the record company, he had to use the tradesmen's entrance. That was the way things were: the black and white artists had to use different doors.

Incidentally, Shirley told me that people often asked her father what he felt about the young European musicians (particularly from Britain) who had taken up his music. She told me that he thought it was a marvellous thing, because they had always given him a credit, made sure everyone knew he had written the original songs. He felt they had taken the seeds of his music and were spreading it all around the world. So he was entirely on their side, which I think is a really great view, given that I am one of the people who have drawn from his work. He didn't say, 'They've ripped me off, and they've made a lot of money from it.' Nothing as mean-spirited as that. To be sure, the Rolling Stones *did* make a lot more money than Willie Dixon. Still, at least he always got the credit and had more recognition and respect in Britain than possibly he got in his own country.

In Europe, people realize what an important part of their musical heritage the blues is. To my mind, jazz and blues music is the only important thing that America has ever come up with. Apart from skyscrapers and Cadillacs. Yes, cars and music and the buildings, but they've done fuck-all else about anything.

Talking of coming up with things, I keep my eyes peeled when I'm travelling for very bad inventions. For instance, throughout Britain and Europe, if you ask for tea in hotels or motorway service areas, it is often served in small metal pots, which all do the same thing. First of all they scald your hand, because the handles are so hot. Next, when you try to pour it, the tea goes all over the table and never in the cup. Now I don't know anybody who hasn't had this experience with them. So the man who designed them presumably got as far as designing the pots, putting the boiling water in them, scalding his hands and spilling it all over the table, and said: 'Right! Let's make six million of these then!'.

Another thing is the hand-drying machine in lavatories. As Mick Talbot, the organ player we sometimes work with, pointed out, it should say: 'Dry hands under the hot air. And then wipe them on your trousers.' That's what you always have to end up doing, as the hot air does absolutely nothing on its own.

And video machines are always put next to the floor instead of on a shelf, at hand or shoulder height, where you could simply reach out and adjust them easily. So to play your video you've got to worship the television before you can even make it work. The world would be ergonomically improved if we could get rid of some of these fiendish faults.

Anyway, we decided to interview Shirley at the window of Chess Records, where there's a large metal silhouette of her father. Geoff thought it would be an idea for him to walk past the window occasionally, as if he was a member of the public. And because he didn't want to look like the same person in every shot, each time he walked by he removed an item of clothing. It was incredibly cold, and by the end he was walking past completely topless, which confused me, and seemed to confuse Shirley a little bit as well. But then he seemed to think this would help the film, and make people think it was a different person each time, rather than just the same raving lunatic removing items of clothing.

I had no idea where either Jimmy Yancey or Albert Ammons had been buried, but in order to make a start on my mission I contacted the Chicago Institute of Jazz History. A very helpful person said they thought Albert's son, Bishop Edsel Ammons, was still living, and he would certainly be able to say where his father was buried. Bishop Ammons was very kind and incredibly helpful (and rather old himself). He was delighted that people had an interest in his father's music, and he directed me to the Lincoln Cemetery.

My idea was to lay a wreath on behalf of all the people in Britain who like Albert's music. He does have a big following. Ian Stuart, the Rolling Stones' pianist, used to love Albert Ammons (and Jimmy Yancey) and he often said to me: '*That's* the stuff that really makes me cry.' And there was a famous London criminal figure called John Binden whom I knew by sight. Once he came up to me in a restaurant, and I was terrified by this towering monster of a man leaning over me. But all he said was, 'You know what I like? I really like that Jimmy Yancey piano. When you play that, that gets me sexy.' So there is an interesting cross-section of people that respond to this type of music. It's a natural music that has an instinctive sort of appeal.

Previous page: The Corn Cob Towers

At first the people in the cemetery office seemed a little confused, until I explained that Albert Ammons was a great and famous pianist. Then they were very helpful. They looked up an old yellow card written in fountain pen, and there was 'Albert Ammons'. Then I suddenly had another idea and asked, 'And is Jimmy Yancey here as well?' Bishop Ammons hadn't been able to tell me whether his father's friend was buried in this cemetery too, but I suspected they might be here together. So they looked him up and found a card for him as well. They told me to go with the gravediggers, who'd show me where he was. I laid the flowers down, and I thought: This is good. This is me showing our respect on behalf of Britain. However, when I looked for Jimmy's grave, I couldn't find it. I had read that when Albert died, Jimmy had played at his funeral; there had been a huge procession of musicians, with Jimmy at its head. So I thought that if he had been buried in the same cemetery, he probably would have been buried near his friend who'd died a few years ahead of him. I asked the gravediggers again, and they showed me where to look: it was only about twenty yards away. But there was just a blank plot, with no headstone. I asked the gravediggers, 'Why isn't there a stone for one of the most important blues pianists in the world?'. And they told me that what probably happened was that the family had spent quite a lot on the funeral (and didn't have much money anyway), and had decided to buy the gravestone later. Then they probably just never got round to it.

I couldn't believe that this man, known and loved in England, whose style can be heard on records from Ray Charles through to the Rolling Stones and myself, could have no memorial stone. So I was very pleased to be in a position to be able to leave one for him. They said it was going to take a few months to make, but it is finished now. That, for me, really made my whole trip worthwhile.

It's important to realize that these people, especially Albert Ammons, were much more than just boogie-woogie pianists. They played all kinds of music. They played stride piano, jazz piano and tunes; they were real pianists. However, they also invented a style which originated in part from the lumber camps.

To understand the history of boogie-woogie music, first we have to look at the deforestation of America. If you look at a map of America in about 1820, 80 per cent of it was covered in woods. But by 1910, only about 20 per cent of it was still wooded – so clearly an incredible amount of deforestation occurred. It was the people that worked in these lumber camps who invented the fast style of blues piano: boogie-woogie. Then people like Jelly Roll Morton and the jazz style of piano-playing made their way up from New Orleans to Chicago with the rural black community from the south travelling to this large industrial city, looking for work. That's how the music travelled up there, and I suppose it peaked in Chicago with Albert Ammons, Pete Johnson and Jimmy Yancey. They then went on to New York, and were hugely successful, household names in the thirties and forties. There was a huge craze for boogie-woogie, which a lot of the big white bands went on to play. Then it kind of shifted into rhythm and blues, and the music changed again, and it moved on from there.

As Chicago was such a big city, it also meant that people would come from all over to play and to listen. For example, Duke Ellington and his orchestra used to play Chicago a lot. Lionel Hampton came from Chicago and Dinah Washington worked here a great deal. In the Prohibition era it was a pretty wild town in general, and that was a magnet for musicians too.

However, on a sourer note, it also happened to be the centre of the musicians' union dispute of the 1940s. The union felt that the people responsible for making records and putting jukeboxes into clubs were going to put musicians out of work. (This was in the days of the big bands, when you needed a lot of musicians to make up a band.) So they actually banned records being made, if you can believe it. For several years in the forties no records were made at all. This, of course, ruined a lot of people's careers, including some of the people I'm talking about here.

Also the musicians' union in Chicago insisted that if there was a radio station playing records, the artists had to put the records on in person. They wouldn't say or do anything on air – they couldn't even pick the record – but they'd have the job of lifting the needle on to it.

Chicago has always been a music city, and the story goes that the word 'jazz' was invented in Chicago, when one of the first jazz bands came up from New Orleans. It was billed as the 'New Orleans Jass Band'. That was how it was supposed to have been spelt. But Chicago has the biggest Polish community outside Poland, and there are a lot of polka bands in the city. So everybody was rushing to see this 'jass' band – they were definitely the most exciting thing happening musically – and the rather put-out polka musicians would cross the J off the 'New Orleans Jass Band', so it would say 'New Orleans Ass Band'. The musicians then changed the spelling to j-a-z-z so the trick wouldn't work any more.

Shoeshine time

Koko Taylor is one of the great blues artists, who came up from the south with her husband in the 1940s, looking for work.

Although Chicago is a very racially divided city, Koko lives in a rather grand suburb. The best thing about her neighbourhood is the landscape gardening. American gardens never seem to have fences, or flowers, or really *anything* of any interest. What they do have is a perfectly cropped lawn, and perhaps an American flag on a pole, and that's it. But in this suburb they had lots of topiary, twirly plants and little pyramid-shaped bushes and all that, which cheered me up no end.

Koko herself was very kind. She showed us round, and her grand-daughter was there playing, and she was very generous in letting us film in her house. She sang a song for us which was kind of saucy and suggestive, all about the butcher coming and wanting to be paid, and how he got paid one way or another. You know, there was a type of innuendo in the music, which I really enjoyed.

As I've said, it's grown-ups' music. It was especially nice and unusual hearing it sung acoustically like that, rather than with the whole band.

Another place we filmed in was Buddy Guy's Club. We had been hoping to film Buddy Guy himself, but unfortunately he was away on tour. I have had the good fortune of working with him, and he is one of the really great bluesmen of the world. However, we *were* able to film Lonnie Brooks, who was very good. Lonnie Brooks has been playing on the blues circuit for a long time, and has worked with such figures as Clifton Chenier and Sam Cooke. His son Ronnie accompanies him and tours with him. So the tradition of passing down a style of the blues through the family has been continued. This is the best way of learning it, being brought up to play it constantly. It is almost impossible to learn it in school.

There is also high culture in Chicago. For instance, they have a huge museum with Old Masters, and paintings by Lucian Freud, the lot. And opposite that museum is where Route 66 starts. I like the way all these things are mashed in together, that's one of the good things about Chicago. They've also got an opera house, and a symphony orchestra directed by Daniel Barenboim. He said, quite rightly, that it doesn't matter how old a piece of music is, it could be five minutes or five hundred years old – that is not relevant. It is whether that piece of music can connect to the listener or not; that's what he is constantly trying to achieve. What matters is whether the music is connected from one person to another.

Reginald Robinson is a young pianist whom I first saw in Chicago about three years ago. At that time he was only about nineteen, and he would have been playing a completely different sort of music to what his friends would be interested in. But he has a natural gift and flair for playing ragtime piano and has written lots of his own music. He's also found unknown pieces by Scott Joplin that were totally lost. It was a treat that he could come and play a piece that he'd written for us. (It was also nice to be doing an item about somebody who wasn't dead.)

The Green Mills Lounge, where we filmed Reginald Robinson, is an extraordinary bar because the interior has remained unchanged since around 1942, when it was redecorated by Steve Brend, who still owns it today. He told me that one of the original owners of the lounge when it first opened in 1907 was the famous gangster Machine Gun Jake McGurn, who had a great deal to do with masterminding the St Valentine's Day Massacre.

There are lots of famous stories about gangsters in Chicago: John Dillinger, for example. In 1934 Dillinger was Public Enemy Number One. The FBI were on his trail. He visited a cinema with a Romanian brothel keeper, who was afraid of being deported by the FBI. She was known as 'the Lady in Red'. The final act of the Dillinger melodrama began at 10.15 p.m., according to the press reports. Dillinger had been watching a gangster film when he stepped out of the Biograph Theater at 2433 Lincoln Avenue. In the doorway of a tavern, two doors south of the movie theatre, stood Melvin Purvis, a federal agent. Dillinger walked right past him; Purvis and two other men followed; then three men closed in from across the street; and two stood at the other end of the alley. Dillinger tried to duck down an alley and pull a gun, but the manhunters beat him to it. They fired. As he died, souvenir hunters rushed over with their handkerchiefs and mopped up his blood. We recreated this in our film, using the original locations, including the Biograph, which hasn't changed in appearance at all.

The city has many gangster-theme restaurants. You'd think, wouldn't you, that in a gangster-theme restaurant people would come round and actually rob the diners? The one I visited was called the Roaring Twenties or something, and people came round dressed as gangsters with pretend

The Wrigley Building

sub-machine-guns while you were having your dinner and pretended to demand money with menaces, or something. It wasn't clear. I don't like this new idea of 'themes' that I've noticed on my travels.

Since Chicago is best-known for crime and music, we went to see Officer Donnie Hixon, who runs a choir made up entirely of policemen and women, the Law and Order Gospel Choir. They have won a lot of competitions, but even when they are practising they all turn up heavily armed. They were singing their songs, and swaying and dancing and clapping, but they all had their guns strapped on. It was quite a strange sight, with their angelic voices expressing peace and harmony, while another message was given out by the Colt 45s in their holsters.

Havana

Cuban music was not something I was particularly well informed about, and I was very keen to go and find out more. Two years ago we had the Buena Vista Social Club on the *Later* programme, with Compay Segundo and Ruben González, and they were great. They were absolutely delightful. They played like from another age, the chords they used and the way they sang songs. There was something charming about the whole thing – the music, the performance, the atmosphere – so I was hoping to find more of that (which, I am pleased to say, I did).

It is always a mistake to have preconceptions about a place before you go, but I did have some. First of all I thought that it was going to be a rather arid and dry place. I also thought it was going to be similar to other Caribbean places I had been to like Jamaica or Antigua, in that it would have mostly rather low-built twentieth-century buildings, with just the occasional older sort of colonial building. I had no preconceptions about the people, although I believed from what I'd heard that they were quite poor there. I knew that cigars were from Cuba, I knew that Castro was its head of state, but other than that I knew very little. So it was a bit hard to tell what the place was going to be like. It had been a very long flight from Chicago via Cancun – endless changes of flights – and I was very tired. So, when we flew in and I looked out of the window, I was delighted to see on first glance that it looked like a cross between Devon and Tennessee. Two places I rather like. It was hilly but with the odd palm tree and with red soil, like Devon. I thought, Well, this is promising … I imagined it was going to be drier somehow. It looked very green and lush.

So once we'd landed at the airport, as I always do, I had a good look round at the airport buildings themselves (and of course at the airport vehicles). The airport seemed, on first impression, to have a character that I could only class as 'Soviet-style concrete'. A rather bossy type of architecture. Modern in the powerful, corporate Eastern Bloc way. We got

The piano's more my style

A great big yellow gondola

through customs and immigration relatively quickly, I'm glad to say – I wouldn't like to have been on the wrong side of the airport authorities here. I think they'd detain you in the airport for a year if they wanted to. But they didn't hassle us, in spite of Geoff's sinister appearance.

I'd heard that there were a lot of old cars in Havana but nothing could have prepared me for the lovely sight in the airport car park of all these 1950s Cadillacs and Chevrolets. And there was something like a 1950s Chevrolet van with its back cut off so as to convert it into a pick-up truck. There was even a single-cylinder Norton ES2 motor cycle with sidecar. All these were in everyday use. I was very surprised to see it all, and it made me realize just how inventive and resourceful the people had to be to keep all these vehicles going. This was before I had even left the airport – I was already impressed.

We drove into Havana along the Malacon, as this long seafront road is called. As we drove to the Nacional Hotel, which is one of the posher hotels there, the first thing I noticed was that Havana had a sort of Torquay flavour to it. This was partly because there were palm trees and big run-down buildings – it had a similar sort of faded charm.

When you first arrive somewhere you're always a bit confused, so I went for a little walk from the hotel to get my bearings. I think you can usually sense the atmosphere on the streets quite quickly – if it's threatening, if it's smart, or if it's poverty-stricken. In Havana, on my first walk, I got the feeling that the people were really quite friendly and just getting on with their lives. I didn't get any bad feelings, which I thought was important.

My preconception about it being a dry place was completely wrong. And so, as it turned out, was my idea that the buildings would mostly be modern. However, I didn't notice this until late in the evening when I went down to old Havana. This area is amazing because it's filled with buildings that the Spanish constructed when they arrived. Columbus was the first European to discover Cuba, and the Spanish subsequently built it up. On reading the history of the place, one finds that it was the centre of the slave trade. Before that an indigenous Indian population lived there, which Columbus recorded as being the most peaceful people he had ever met. Anyway, they were wiped out by the Spanish. It made me realize again how powerful Spain had been – obviously one of the biggest world powers there was. And, as we were to find out when we went there, Seville was a powerful port city for Spain during the bad old slaving days, so there is quite a direct link from it to Cuba. The result of this is that there is now a rather pretty old town with beautiful sixteenth-century Spanish buildings. The atmosphere and buildings reminded me of Siena or somewhere else in Italy. A southern European look, I suppose, but stuck in a subtropical climate. And the atmosphere of the place, with these cars literally being held together so they grind along – they don't whoosh along, they grind along – all this made it rather romantic; it added to the charming, crumbling feel of the place.

So when I arrived I didn't really know what to expect at all. I knew there would be good music, I knew there would be good cigars, but the more I looked at the place the more I liked it. It's true that a lot of the inhabitants want to leave it, but, in fact, having come from a rather cold Chicago, I concluded that if you were poor (as most people in Havana are) you'd probably be better off living in Havana than you would be living in Chicago.

The first job in a film is to select how you are going to get about. If you're going to walk you'll be rather limited in the amount that you can see and take in. But of course if you're in an open-top car you can drive around with a camera peering out and the camera can see every-thing easily. So when we got to Havana I decided that an old American car was probably the right thing, the obvious choice really. The only choice. In the end we chose a beautiful bright yellow Cadillac, a 1949 convertible.

When the Mafia were in cahoots with the dictator, Batista, whom Castro had ousted, they had brought in all these really glamorous cars – like the Jaguar XK120 or the Dusenberg to name just a few – cars that were relatively untouched. They're supposed to be in a museum in Havana somewhere. There was some talk about trying to borrow one of these, but we realized there might be difficulties getting hold of one, so in the end we just borrowed the Cadillac.

I had been very impressed with the huge selection of cars we had to choose from, but I was pleased with the one we got. It was like a great big yellow gondola to get into. It had a large silver swan mascot on it (which is in fact the correct one). I think it was quite a rare car, certainly in Havana. It was definitely the only one there and, anyway, a Cadillac is one of the most prestigious of American cars. I think it can be said to be the Rolls-Royce of American cars. Also we could all fit into it, which was a bonus.

Osvaldo (whose car it was) was very reluctant at first to allow me to have a go. But when I showed him photographs of the cars I had in London, and asked him the right sort of questions, like was it a

three-speed box and things like that, he realized that I was a car-head, and said it would be all right for me to drive it. I assured him that I would treat it like it was my own baby and after that he seemed to relax. Osvaldo is a mechanic, and of course a car of that age which has been serviced by one man has all sorts of little eccentricities that you have to master. Which he kindly showed me. You know, ways of operating the brakes so they don't fail.

When you check in to your hotel room, if you turn the television on, or listen to the radio, it will tell you a great deal about the country you're in (unless of course you're watching Sky or BBC World Service or something, which is the same the world over). But in Cuba the radio is entirely state run, and I didn't really listen to it at all. Partly because I couldn't make much sense of it, to be honest. But anyway, in our opening link we decided it would be nice to suggest the radio as a useful thing for understanding the local culture: a shot of myself supposedly turning on the car radio and nodding along with the song, but then pulling back to reveal a live band in the back of the car. We wanted the band to do a typical Cuban song, and probably the most famous Cuban song is 'Guantanamera'. A lot of people think (I thought so myself) that it came from South America – but in fact it's Cuban. The band we used for this was the one we found playing in the hotel bar; I don't even know their name, but they were very good. They were playing 'Guantanamera', which is a sort of Cuban national folk song, but what was interesting was that their version was different to the one I'd grown up with. They used slightly different chords – I guess theirs are the right ones. So in the versions that *we* hear on the radio, the sort of pop hit versions of it, the chords have been changed from the original.

However, Osvaldo showed a little concern when he saw them all climbing into the back of his car with their instruments. There were four of them and to be able to film them we had to have them sitting above the back seat. I could see a little look on his face which told me that

Osvaldo was probably thinking: Mm. If he's treating my car like it's a baby, why is he letting these people tread all over its face? But fortunately he spoke to them, and they removed their shoes – which weren't too smelly or anything at all, I'm pleased to say. After that he was perfectly all right about it. I think. He could see what we were trying to do. And anyway, they sat very delicately on the car.

The earliest inhabitants of Cuba were Indians, although I think, out of the various Indians living there, one tribe was always chasing another tribe out. In fact, there were always people being chased out of Cuba from the very earliest of times, as far as history records. And then Columbus came in 1492 and he recorded in his diary how lovely the people were. He wrote these words about them: 'They are the best people in the world, without knowledge of what is evil, nor do they murder or steal. All the people show the most singular loving behaviour and are gentle and are always laughing.'

He wrote all that, about the people being so nice, but in spite of this (or maybe because of it) they were pretty soon wiped out by the slave traders. At one point they politely went out to meet the awful invaders, just to greet them and be friendly, and what happened? They were all killed. They were just massacred. Pretty rough times were had.

Of course, during the slave trade, the slaves were unloaded and had to work in the fields in Cuba, and that was pretty unpleasant for them all. There was one famous slave leader who was burnt at the stake by the Spanish. They said to this leader, 'Well, before you die, would you like to give your confession to the Catholic priest?' And he said, 'Well, is the Catholic priest Spanish?' So they said, 'Yes.' 'And are all these people burning me Spanish?' So they said, 'Yes.' 'So if I make my confession to him I might go to heaven – the same place he's going?' So again, the answer was yes. So he said, 'Well I don't want to go there. If all these awful people are there, it's going to be hell.' I think this man is regarded as a saint in Havana now.

I'm a car-head and treated it like my own baby

Another interesting fact is that Nelson also visited Cuba – this is some years later, of course. Nelson visited with William IV, or the prince who had yet to become William IV. This was the king who was to be known as 'Silly Billy' because he was pretty hopeless, disagreeing with the government on everything and being unhelpful. When Nelson visited Havana with him, he immediately tried to marry a local girl. Nelson managed to get him out of it, and dragged him away in time. In the middle of all this Nelson wrote back to King George saying what a great man his son was, how everyone loved him and that he was doing everything just fine. A complete bare-faced lie showing Nelson's loyalty to Prince William.

Anyway, I found the drive round the streets of Havana to be very pleasant: the drivers were friendly, if enthusiastic, and somehow there was a feeling of old-fashioned courtesy. Even Osvaldo's loud car horn (which I had occasion to use quite frequently) sounded rather good-humoured. It seemed to be the embodiment of the Cuban personality and temperament; it wasn't 'GET OUT OF MY WAY!', it was 'Excuse me, please. Thank you; it's a nice day, isn't it?'

Ports always seem to have a lively and seedy feel to them, and Havana was no exception. It surrounds a huge natural harbour which the British ran at one point, until we swapped it with America for a couple of sacks of tea or something. They put a huge chain under the harbour, which is about half a mile across. You tighten it up and it stops ships coming in or going out.

In 1956 Castro and his friend Che Guevara returned to the island in a boat called *Granma*, only to find Batista waiting for them. Many rebels were killed in the fight that followed, but Castro and Che both managed to escape to the hills. From there they made more and more successful raids against Batista and his forces, which of course earned them enormous popularity.

But before all that the port was at one time Pirate Central. It was where all the pirates in the Caribbean hung out. Mary Reed, the

famous girl-pirate from London, who dressed as a man for years, spent quite a long time in Havana with other cut-throats. It must have been quite a romantic place at that time, and you can still almost smell a bit of that about it all. So to get a feel for it, I decided to park the car and walk for a bit.

At the port is the bar where Ernest Hemingway used to hang out a lot. I think he used to go down there and have a whale of a time and, in between writing his books, get pissed, get tarts, get drugs. That's what they say. I don't know if it's true or not. You can't tell about these things without having been there.

I did notice that walking around generally people were really friendly, and also it was one of the most integrated places I have ever been, racially speaking. There were Spanish people, African-looking people, there were Syrian-looking people – all different types. Partly this is because it was a trading port where people came in and out, and then slaves were left there. It isn't as if there is a black part of town or a white part of town or a Spanish part of town. It was all just mixed up, as far as I could see. Maybe if you lived there you'd notice the differences, but you really didn't feel any sense of segregation, unlike in other towns. For example, in Chicago all the black people live in one place and all the white people live in another place. In most places this seems to be the case. I didn't get the feeling, when walking around, that I stood out particularly (obviously apart from my stunning looks).

Havana is probably more pleasant to visit nowadays if you're a tourist, because now there are shops and you can go and buy a cup of coffee, which you couldn't do before. But the other thing that I noticed while I was walking around was that, like so many other places, people always say, 'If you'd only been here twenty years ago …' People always talk about the past nostalgically – and the figure they pick about countries is usually twenty years: 'Oh, twenty years ago – that was when it was still lovely; it's a pity you couldn't have visited it *then*.' Smug bastards. But it seemed pretty good now to me and I'm sure in twenty years' time from now it will be: 'Oh it was *great* when Jools was filming here, you know, that was when it was still so unspoilt.' I suppose I can say that to my children when they plan a visit here some time in the year 2018.

As I was leaving the port area I saw little things, some of which weren't caught on film. For instance, there were ships leaving the harbour, and children were swimming in the water almost alongside these ships. They would jump from the road right into the water; the ships go by about fifty or sixty yards from the bank. There was a sailor on the deck of one ship which was going off, and there was a woman with a baby running after it waving goodbye; she just kept running following the ship. He was waving goodbye and she was in tears and he was in tears, and I thought how charming it was. I don't think he was deserting her, it was just a sort of long-drawn-out farewell. However, it doesn't resemble my own farewells to my family. I sometimes say goodbye but that's as far as I go. Otherwise I leave a note about what time I might be returning and what I want to eat that night.

Apart from the band in the back of the car, the first piece of music we filmed was the Buena Vista Social Club, who as I said were the ones we had on *Later* with Ry Cooder. We decided we wanted to film them in Havana Square. It's a big square of the sort you'd get in an old European town, but what lent it its charm was that it was so falling-down and that there were still families living in all of the buildings. Washing was hanging out and some of the windows were blocked up and everything was propped up with wood. They were recobbling the square and I think if anything it will become the posh district soon, as was the way with slums like Notting Hill in London.

In the square we asked Compay Segundo and Ruben González to perform. Ruben is eighty-two, and Compay is in his nineties. Ruben played the piano for us throughout the programme; he's a brilliant pianist. His theory is that you should just play all the time, then if it's being recorded or being filmed you can capture it, but he's just playing all the time anyway, or thinking about music at least. In listening to him play you're hearing the entire history of the Cuban piano style. He's not only one of the carriers of that tradition but also the inventor of his own style. So when you hear him it really sums up everything that is Cuban music.

And he was charming. But we immediately ran into a problem with the piano. We wanted to film Ruben in the square first on his own and then together with Compay Segundo. We got the piano people to bring the piano to the square, and I went to check it before he arrived. It was a baking hot day and the sun was beating down on all of us, and the piano didn't work. It was just this completely beaten-up old crap piano that the worst pub pianist would have walked away from. So I said: 'Well, this isn't very good, we've got to try to get him another piano.' So I went with Geoff and one of the researchers, and a translator, to try to find a better one. Somebody said there's a bar round the corner and it's got a grand piano in it. So we walked five minutes round the corner and found a bar, which was one of the state-run sort of coffee bars. Cuban people don't like you going into some of these bars because they're very cheap – it would be a bit unfair because the tourists are so much richer. And it would be no good charging a tourist fifty pence for a cup of coffee when they're only charging the locals one penny for it. The same way you get the tea bars for the taxi drivers in London.

So anyway, this was one of those state-run places, quite a grand place, and it had a grand piano. We said to the man in charge: 'Look, we are desperate,' and explained what the situation was. However, we got what I could call a little bit of the old Cuban mentality. This is a thing that goes hand in hand with Communism, I think. Because people get paid the same whatever they do, they tend to have a certain inflexibility. He said: 'No way can you move the piano.' We said, 'We'll pay a thousand dollars if we can borrow the piano.' And he still said no. We had put it in such a way that we offered to pay the money first 'to the premises', but he

Ruben González

said he was just the manager and couldn't take responsibility. We said, 'Well, you just take the money and sort it out later,' in other words offering it as a bribe – but no, he didn't want it. His job was to run a bar. He wasn't there to think about renting out pianos. Even though we were offering him $1000, which he could have pocketed, and we said we'd lift it round there and lift it back, he didn't want to know. Because it was something he just didn't want to have to think about. In other words, he was unbribable and incorruptible and a completely useless git.

In the end, we were stuck with the crap piano, so when Ruben González arrived I said, 'I'm really sorry about the piano. What should we do?' We only had the one morning in which to capture the thing; we didn't have time to look around for somewhere else. We were stuck. Anyway, Ruben sat down and started to play the piano and I asked him, 'Well, what do you think?' He said, 'This piano is shit,' and I said, 'I know.' He then said, 'Mind you, I've played much worse so we'll just make do with it.' Which he did. Very nice of him. So he made do with this very poor piano and made it sound all right.

The other thing that was interesting is that he played quite boldly on his own but when Compay Segundo turned up he suddenly went much more quiet and introverted. This was because Compay is the older man and in groups you always get that. For instance, even if somebody is just two or three years younger than the others, this person will always be the baby of the group. With most people, if there is a few years' age gap that is noticeable when you're young, it usually fades and disappears once you are in your twenties. But for some reason, in bands, this age gap always remains. That's what happened with these two musicians. Because Compay is the older (and maybe slightly more well-known man), Ruben went all quiet and sort of in the background, respectful of his 'elder' even though they're both now old and respected and to us seem to be the same age.

While they were playing in the square, there were some dancers there who moved so beautifully, they were like statues that twirled. They were just stunning – I've never seen anything like it. And they were all ages, these dancers. There were people of, say, seventeen and seventy, all doing the same dance together. I thought this was a very encouraging thing. In the same way that when you walk around the streets there are people of all races blending in, it was nice to see all ages dancing together, all liking the same sort of music. I think it shows that, although there are bad things about Cuba, they are just about outweighed by all the good things about it. The good thing in this instance is that commercialization probably hasn't got to them. It's only because of the way people advertise goods that we think, Oh, I'm a young person, so I'll buy this. Or, I'm an old person, so I'll buy that. Whereas if you don't have that thrust upon you, you probably just find that you all like the same thing. Which is why there were people of all ages dancing to their music. Although their two leaders have a joint age of 170, the band will play with people who are in their twenties and there was even a small child in the square who liked singing Compay's songs; she was about seven years old. Communism might kill initiative on the one hand – as with the stubborn git in the bar, refusing to be bribed – but on the other it somehow stops people being sold a lot of crap most of the time.

If you looked up the definition of a true gent, Compay Segundo fits it. He smoked a cigar and was larger than life, wore a hat, laughed in a loud and clear manner, sang and enjoyed himself. That seemed to me to be the reason he'd grown to be so old – along with the nice Cuban climate, of course.

We were very keen to speak to Fidel Castro, or Dr Castro as he's sometimes called. Or General Castro. Whatever takes his fancy. He has been there, after all, in control in a rather unusual way for the last forty years, so he can call himself anything he likes. However, we were unable to get an interview, I regret to say, or even an audience.

Overleaf: all ages dancing together

When we checked into the Nacional Hotel, there was a bit of a kerfuffle going on and it turned out that the two supermodels, Kate Moss and Naomi Campbell, were staying there. I was very pleased, because they are friends of mine; I thought, That's marvellous. So I rang them and asked them if they wanted to pop out for something to eat or drink that evening. They said, 'We'll see you for a drink later but can't join you for dinner because we've got a prior engagement.' I thought, What! somebody better than me? How can this be true? But it turned out they'd arranged to meet Castro himself, or that Castro had asked to meet them. I did think momentarily, What can they possibly have that I haven't got, that Castro would be interested in? ... and then, it came to me – it was a lady's perspective of England which they could share with him, which I would not have been able to do.

Anyway, I joined them for drinks afterwards to try to find out second-hand what he was like. They said they had had a marvellous time, and said he was the kindest, wittiest, funniest, most charmingly persuasive man they had ever met. They were staying in the Churchill Suite of the Nacional Hotel and just because they'd had dinner with Castro extra care was taken; they were supplied with whatever they needed. And I was seen as a person who was a friend of somebody that Castro had had dinner with; I was treated with great respect from then on. (Although I had been treated perfectly well before then anyway.)

My only regret about not managing to force my way along with them was that I could have said to him: 'If you're just on your own, Mr Castro, aren't you going to feel a bit of a gooseberry? If I'm there it'll even the whole thing out.'

So, in honour of Dr Castro, we stayed up late into the night and had a lovely party. We drank many toasts to Castro's health because he'd given Naomi and Kate such a nice time.

Luckily, the next day started off in rather a relaxed manner as we were all feeling a little tired after our celebratory evening. Geoff had sensibly arranged for us to film some music on the beach. It was of a thirteen-piece band named Hanny, led, as it happens, by a musician named Hanny. They were rehearsing. As musicians are paid for by the state, they must rehearse when the state says, and even do gigs where the state says. It would be a bit like in Britain depending upon the Civil Service to be your agent, your manager and your record producer, and I wouldn't fancy that much. But here in Cuba, the state trains them, and gives them gigs, and everybody gets paid the same (which isn't a great deal). It doesn't matter if you work in a cigar factory or what, everybody gets paid the same.

Wherever you go there are monuments to Che Guevara, who was Castro's closest companion in the early days of the revolution, and pictures of him as well. In Revolution Square there is this one vast tower which can be see from everywhere, and I really did think if people came back in 2 million years' time – no, not 2 million years' time, if people came back in a thousand years' time to planet Earth – they would certainly wonder what it was, whether it was some great religious temple or what. It's built in what I would describe as 1950s Soviet 'power architecture'. It had a certain charm to it, really.

Revolution Square is also the place where Castro makes his speeches. Now, Mr Castro is renowned for his nice long speeches. The last one went on for seven hours. Indeed the soundman who was with us had got the job of doing the sound for a big interview with Mr Castro. He showed me a photograph of the people who went with him, and it was all very respectable – people with ties on who were from the BBC, CNN, NBC news and one other news company. Four of them going to interview Castro about one particular thing. But when they arrived in Havana, they were told that only one of them would be allowed to talk to Castro. There was a big argument about who it was going to be – Ted Turner himself, from CNN, became involved, then the chairman of the BBC, saying: 'No, *we* should do it', and eventually it was agreed that Mr . . . would do it – I can't even remember which one it was, and that the BBC crew would be used. After all this the person who was finally chosen went into the room to interview Mr Castro, asked his first question and Mr Castro then spoke for an hour non-stop – and that was the end of the interview. So I do like the sound of him. I don't think he's a crashing bore either, probably quite funny.

As it happens I've been wondering what question I would have asked him had I ever got my audience, and, to tell you the truth, I'm not sure *what* I would have asked him. I know what I wouldn't have asked him. Some people say he deliberately keeps things tricky with America, because then America becomes the focus of the Cubans' resentment and blame. So if they didn't have that they might start blaming *him* for some of the things that don't work around here. I wouldn't have asked him about that because I think he would have shown me the door. But I would have asked him what he thought of people who *had* that view (making it clear that it wasn't me that had that view), what he thought of them. Of people who had a *stupid* view like that – what would he do to them? Maybe he'd have shown me the cells where people who had that type of view would be put, and what exactly would happen to them in there. Now that would certainly make a very good interview.

A lot of the people love Castro because of what he's done for health and education in Cuba – yes, the people certainly love him for that. The same way that people resent him for not letting them be Catholic or gay. Although I think he's eased up on all of that now.

Next, I would have asked him about the attempts on his life. The CIA, in league with the Mafia, thought it would be a good idea to get rid of him, and it appears they tried some fairly mad ways. First they discovered that he was a great fan of skin-diving, so they sent him, as a gift, a skin-diving suit, the inside of which was coated with lethal chemicals that would have given him a dreadful disease of the skin and killed him off. But he was suspicious and never put it on. Next they sent him an exploding seashell (again, as a gift), but it went off out at sea. Then they coated his shoes with a vicious chemical when he was staying in New York at the UN, which was meant to make his hair drop out. Their reasoning was that once his beard dropped out he would surely lose all credibility. They stuck stuff in his cigars which would have made him hallucinate slightly, and therefore talk gibberish – which was also meant to make him lose credibility with his people. They even considered the idea of getting a hitman in, but they couldn't figure out how a hitman would get out of Cuba alive. They tried various methods of poisoning, but it never worked, it always backfired. They even tried dropping leaflets saying '$10,000 for anyone who kills Castro'. And that went on for years. To this day, I've been told, he has fifty-two houses, one for every week, and you never know which one he's going to be in (unless you're Kate or Naomi).

One of the things I was interested in, in coming to Havana, was that it is the most famous cigar-manufacturing place in the world – Mr Castro himself has given up cigars after what was described as a 'heroic struggle'. The cigar factories are all in Havana, and when they were taken over by the state they kept the names the same as when they were family-run businesses. Almost all the different names and brands of cigars are – oddly enough – made in the same factories. What is really interesting is that out of all the cigars they make here, they only export about 20 per cent.

The cigars you get here are delicious. I used to smoke cigars a long time ago. When I was first with Squeeze I used to smoke cheap ones, and then I started to smoke cigarettes. It's very hard to kick the habit of cigarettes; however, eventually I did, and I didn't smoke anything for a few years. Now I just have one cigar a day, and I find that the Havana cigar is a treat. It's true what they say, that the reason Havana is best is because of the robustness of the leaf it produces: the soil in Havana makes the best tobacco leaf. Nobody is really quite sure why the best wine comes out of certain vineyards in France or the best wood for a Stradivarius violin comes from certain woods in Germany; it's the same thing with Havana soil.

While we were waiting to film the last sequence, I met a charming woman who chatted to me for a bit. She was smoking a cigar (and that is another great thing – everybody, even all the old ladies, smokes cigars), and she said it is very important to have a nice cup of coffee with a cigar. She also told me that her son had moved to England, but he doesn't like the weather there and he's become very depressed and unhappy and he won't go out. He also can't buy Havana cigars there. I thought, how sad: just knowing that he was there and that he was unhappy and that she missed him a great deal. It made me realize that, although Cuba is a poor country, in some ways the inhabitants are indeed rich. For example, they have nice weather, good music and can smoke an incredible amount of cigars.

I wanted to buy some cigars to take home, but they are not cheap in the factory, indeed they are not a lot cheaper than what they cost in London. For instance, a particular box might be $200 here in Havana, where it may be £200 in London. You can buy outside on the streets, but we were told not to buy them off people in the street, who make completely phoney ones. (I did once buy a box of what they call 'snide' ones, which in fact look identical to the real thing: the box is identical, the label is identical. However, when you come to smoke them it's like smoking a piece of rope – practically impossible.) Instead you find somebody who has a contact and can get the real thing cheap. The people who work in the cigar factories get about ten dollars a month, or something, but they get given a few free cigars, and also take out a few if they really want, and, more importantly, they can take the leaves with them. And when you look at how they make cigars, they literally just get the leaves, roll them up, put them into an old wooden press, leave them for a while, cut the ends off and that's a cigar. They can easily take the leaves home and make them themselves. And they do. The ones they make at home are identical to the ones they are making in the factory. They will make up a box and sell those for $50, which is five months' wages, and also make a profit. So you're getting the same thing, they're getting money themselves, and everybody's happy (except the state, of course, who are getting fiddled out of their cigar revenue). That's the way one should buy cigars, I was told. If that's what you're after. I was; so I did.

Then we were off to a slightly smarter part of town where a lot of the embassies are located. We wanted to speak to the British Ambassador to ask him what our official policy was here in Cuba, but he didn't seem to have the time to talk to us.

The most fantastic of the embassies, indeed the most fantastic building that I actually saw in Cuba, is the Russian Embassy. It is on this street full of rather grand villas which are all embassies. You go past the German Embassy, which is a big colonial-looking villa. Next you go past the Dutch Embassy, which is a modern type of villa, but still a traditional enough looking building, and *then* you get to it. An area is fenced off – it must be three, four, maybe even six acres. First a huge fence, and next this building which looks like a giant rocket ship that has crashed headlong into the ground. It is a powerful and terrifying concrete Soviet building which looks like a badly designed cathedral; it is very strangely flared upwards in its construction. On the very top there seems to be an observation tower, with people looking at everything everybody's doing, and also listening to what everybody is thinking and saying. Below, it looks as though there is one vast room, where a James Bond villain sits stroking a white cat on his lap. He's looking at maps of the world, seeing where world leaders are going to gather, and working out how he can threaten and blackmail them into giving him all of their money (or whatever people like that get up to). I do think for a building to express all that means it really has been a complete success, and I think that is exactly what they were trying to express when they built it. They certainly weren't trying to say, 'We're all jolly, warm, friendly and touchie-feelie.' Very different from the place which was once the headquarters of the despotic old ruler Batista. That has been turned into

a museum celebrating the revolution, and a very jolly place it is too. It even has a Soviet tank in the corner. But once Castro had overthrown Batista his problems weren't over, because the Americans took against him. In fact so much so that they invaded at the Bay of Pigs. And then, because the Cubans had Russian missiles here, they took even more against him, and imposed an embargo. This meant that effectively nothing could come in or out (which is why they have the fantastic old cars).

The Americans don't have an embassy, but they do have a building called the Trade Center, or something like that, and opposite it there is a great big poster for the revolution – it's all in Spanish so the Americans won't be able to make head or tail of it.

I think it was very difficult for Cuba when the Soviet Bloc started to fall apart, because they depended upon the Russians so much. It's been quite hard for them since. There is, ironically, a two-thirds-scale perfect copy of the Capitol building in America which was built in the 1930s, and it has the Cuban flag flying on top of it.

After we'd driven around all afternoon looking at monuments and embassies, Geoff suddenly had to be taken to hospital. I'm sure it was just the heat, and had nothing to do with our delightful evening discussing Mr Castro with Kate and Naomi. Anyway, he got to discover first-hand what the Cuban medical system was like. He said it was excellent. And, unlike somewhere like Chicago, absolutely free. Geoff was particularly pleased about this aspect, I feel. They were so good that the next day he was back with us, ready (although not that willing) to visit the famous dance school.

One of the researchers suggested that we visit this dance school set up by Laura Alonso, who is the daughter of one of Cuba's leading ballerinas. Like many things in Cuba it is totally underfunded, but everything is still done rather well. The commitment by all the parents to the school and to getting things done there is so impressive. It is in one of the poorest neighbourhoods of Havana, and all these little Havana slum children come to it. As I walked around with Laura they would curtsy to her, perfectly mannered. They also bowed to me. When I asked her why she'd set it up she just answered, 'For them,' gesturing in a graceful way to all the young children there waiting to perform for us.

The way they dance is so advanced for their years: dancers of eight or nine are performing routines that wouldn't be expected of fourteen- or fifteen-year-old European children. It was incredible to see. And moving to see their ballet shoes all worn out and ill-fitting, and costumes which they had made themselves. Because, of course, there is no money at all. There is a very cheap cassette recorder that plays music for them to dance to, and I staggered into a room to see this amazing sight. Although normally they do classical ballet, there happened to be a version of a song, 'It's Crying Time Again', playing on the cassette machine, and these two children were dancing, and it was just fantastic. The music was really crackling, which only added to the charm. Even now, as I write, I find it difficult to hold back the tears.

Before we went to film at the ballet school, Geoff wasn't at all enthusiastic about including it. He was saying things like, 'What do we know about ballet and dance? … It's all a bit poncy, isn't it?' but by the time we left he was just like me, his lower lip was trembling and his eyes were watering, because it was such a beautiful thing to see these people doing this. In the face of the hardest odds, people could still make beauty.

The other great dancers we observed in Cuba were the boxers in training. The former Olympic heavyweight champion, Teofilo Stephenson, has a school in another part of Havana, also a very poor part of town. He trains young boys from the age of eight upwards. Teofilo was one of the greatest boxers of all time. He was never professional, so never won the world championship, but for three Olympic Games running he beat everybody. He was just unbeatable. Everybody said if he had become professional and moved to America (which he had had the opportunity to do), he would have become incredibly rich and successful. Yet instead of choosing to do that, he stayed in Havana. When I asked him why, he said it was because he could exercise his mind in Havana, which in America he couldn't. It was a mindless country. That was his view.

I also asked him who was the toughest opponent that he had ever fought against. And he said: 'Training.' At which point Geoff went: 'Oh, yeah, right,' and he really seemed to agree with this statement. It was a point that I felt Geoff understood. It is the biggest opponent any of us has to face, training, or indeed (if you're Geoff) working.

The cars that we go around in here are these huge hulking dinosaurs, and people use everything they can find to keep them on the road. They put Soviet jeep engines or diesel engines inside them, just to keep them going. They use simply anything they can get their hands on. They don't have these big beautiful cars because they're aesthetically pleasing; they have them because they're the only cars they've got. It does make the place look like a 1940s film set.

On a couple of occasions I couldn't get an official taxi, but someone would take you if you just gave them money. They would take you in their car, and it turns out they've used honey instead of brake fluid, and things like that. They make things up. Their imaginative resources really have to be saluted. I think that English car restorers and the classic car movement really have to take their hats off to these car owners here in Cuba, because with nothing they've managed to keep these cars going. Because of the climate, the cars are all quite well preserved. When they're repainted, it has all been done by hand, so you can see the brush stokes. That's OK really, because they serve the purpose, which is to get people around.

Being a person who fancies himself as a bit of a time traveller and wondering what it would be like to be in such and such a street fifty or a hundred years ago, or something like that, it was suddenly like having gone back in time. A lot of these cars are about fifty years old. I suppose it is also a credit to the original American manufacturers, because they were certainly built to do a lot of miles and all that. Seeing the cars was something I really enjoyed. It always made me feel that I was on holiday.

Geoff, I must say, gets incredibly bored with all my car talk. Myself and Andy Matthews, who is the editor of the film, were looking at a classic car magazine and we realized that one of the most overlooked cars, which we spotted in Havana (and were very surprised to see), was a Morris Marina. It was what I would call a rogue car, and I believe that one or two English cars did get to Cuba. At one point we saw a Singer Gazelle, and Andy and I couldn't stop talking about this – seeing a 1950s Rootes' Group vehicle made in Britain in the 1950s parked here in Havana. And, you know, I think Geoff said something like 'Fuckin' hell, you're boring,' or that sort of remark. But still, it was very nice to see it. There were one or two other unusual sightings of English vehicles. For example, the Norton ES2 motor cycle. There was a Rover 2000, an Austin 1100. Of course the reason there are all these really glamorous cars is because in the 1950s the Mafia ran Cuba along with this man Batista. They had all these celebrities and other glamorous people coming into the casinos, so they needed really flash cars. The big nobs had these cars

sort of locked away in garages and there are supposed to be some real treasures still here dating from that time. Actually that's another regret about not seeing Castro, because he could have told us where all the decent motors were hiding. He himself drives a Mercedes Benz, I believe.

Geoff: 'Fucking hell, you really *are* a boring twat.'

In the narrow streets of old Havana, especially in the evenings, the tropical heat makes it feel like another era. You go into these bars and you can imagine them full of pirates, or gangsters, or professional revolutionaries. I went into a bar there and a man came up to me and said, 'Ah – you are the great ac-tor,' and I thought: 'Ello, he obviously doesn't know who I am. I told him, 'Well, I'm not, actually,' and he said, 'No, no! You're much too modest! I am a humble teacher and I will tell you something of Cuban history.' So I said: 'All right, but I'm really not an actor although it's very kind of you to say so, but if you've got a bit of history, I'd love to hear it.' Then there was no shutting him up for about two hours. He was such a nice man, but I can't remember a word of what he said. To console myself against this droning barrage I followed the advice of Artur Rubinstein and ordered a coffee and a drink and lit up my cigar. He had said: 'No lover of cigars can imagine the voluptuous pleasure of sitting in a café, sipping slowly a strong magnificent coffee, and smoking rhythmically those divine leaves of Cuba.'

Then we went to this other bar, which we found had a band, which kind of captures the atmosphere of what it was like in Havana; people dance, they have a nice time, they're kind of fiery. When I walked into the bar, there was a sailor, who recognized me when I brushed past him, and he said hello to me. Maybe he thought I was that actor too. Anyway, this bar reminded me of an old-fashioned dock town, which are disappearing more and more – towns gathered round a harbour and everything working around that – and that's what Havana still is.

Grooving with the Afro-Cuban rhythm section

The women are pretty in Cuba – there is something about the spirit and the character of them – and the men are really handsome, too. They are an attractive people and they're very mixed. As I said earlier, the indigenous population of Indians was wiped out in the 1600s, as they were too nice. So there really isn't an indigenous population left. Today's Cubans are all descended from people who have visited, from slaves, people who worked for the Spanish, or pirates. That's where they all come from, and they do have a certain look and smile and character which are 'large'.

Because people have no money prostitution is quite rife, and there are girls standing along the seafront sort of hitchhiking. It's a bit confusing, because people hitchhike lifts from one another, anyway. It's perfectly acceptable here. There are both girls and boys working as prostitutes, and because they have so little money, and the exchange rate isn't very good for them, I think there are probably sex tourists here. If the average wage in Cuba is $10 a month and the average wage in a European country is $1000 a month, a difference like that obviously encourages odd behaviour. We talked to a prostitute but there wasn't too much to say, I thought, because the story sort of spoke for itself. She had an incredible smile. I think it's a shame that basically prostitution is there for one reason and one reason only, to get money, and that's her reason: she needed money. She told us her views, which were quite interesting, about who was the best in bed and who was the worst.

I began the conversation by saying to her: 'What do you do?' She said: 'Well, usually I'll get somebody, and I tell them, "Take me out for a drink, take me out for dinner, let's go dancing,"' and then eventually they would have sex. It seemed a bit like the long way round to me. I didn't know it was such a long-drawn-out affair. Incredibly expensive as well. You know, dancing, dinner, and blimey.

But, anyway, when I asked which nationality she preferred, she said that the Spanish were the best, and she quite liked Frenchmen, but the English were definitely the worst. I still don't really know if she meant that they were the worst payers, or the worst at taking a girl out, or maybe they were the worst dancers, or maybe they had the worst eating manners.

Geoff: 'The worst shaggers, she meant.'

Yes, or maybe the worst shaggers. I don't know; but I wish her well. And although there is a lot of prostitution in Havana, I wouldn't say it is the main feature of the place. Having said that, it *has* always been there. It was known as the 'Brothel of the Caribbean' in the eighteenth century. It has always had a reputation as being a bit of a risqué place.

We had a translator but the translator asked her a question, she would answer her in Spanish, and then instead of telling us what the answer was, the translator would go on to talk to her some more in Spanish. Just chatting, really. They just went on chatting for quite a while.

There were some chords I learnt while I was in Havana, which I heard played by Rubén González. A double-bass player called Cachaito López, who's played on all the great Cuban records, told me what they were. These chords summed up what Havana was to me. They were rather intriguing because at first you think, once you've heard them, that you know what they are, but then you need to hear them again. It's just this little sequence of chords, and in the end I even wrote them down on a piece of manuscript. And if you ask a lot of the great songwriters what they like about music most of them will say, 'The changes.' This is what this is, a set of changes. You know, you take five chords, and the way that they change, from one chord to the next, that's what music is really.

Chucho Valdez is one of the greatest Latin jazz pianists of all time. It was marvellous playing with him because, although he hardly spoke any English at all, when we played a duet together we communicated in exactly the same language. I think it was another example of how music is a common language. He and I could talk to one another without being able to say a word, which is kind of magical really. We played a version of 'Blue Monk', because we both like Thelonius Monk, the American pianist.

A beautiful square in the Spanish governor's house – but it's hot.
Cachaito (above) on his double bass, and (right) Des'ree.

People visit Cuba all the time for different purposes, and we discovered that Des'ree was in Havana making two videos. As she was there, we wondered whether she would like to do something with us. So she got together with the Afro-Cuban rhythm section, who played percussion, and the bass player Cachaito. I asked her what song she wanted to do, and she mentioned various songs, and then suddenly she said, '"Something".' She didn't know it was a George Harrison song, and was thrilled to learn it was – and it worked out. We went through it maybe four or five times and filmed the sixth time once we'd worked it out and that was it. Spontaneity. And for me that sums up Cuba as well – because Cuba is quite a spontaneous place. It's not about hanging about. Although you're poor, there's nothing to say you have to be miserable and unhappy. Although people obviously do want to be more comfortable, and be better off, they don't seem to let it get them down. They're not gloomy, and you can see that in their music and in their temperament. There's something optimistic about them, which is rather warming.

All this took place in the front of a museum. There is a courtyard which fronts on to the square in the old part of Havana. It was a simply beautiful square: there was the Spanish governor's house which he built in 1710 or something, a really beautiful building with these rooms off it, which is where we chose to film. At one point we had to stop filming because there were some Russian dignitaries coming round, and there's Geoff; he was bridling. He was saying things like, 'Don't they realize that Jools and Des'ree are far more dignified than these bloody digs, and more important,' and glaring at them. It was all very good because the Russians couldn't speak a word of English and couldn't understand anything of what he was saying about them.

The lovely thing about Havana is that it has a certain mystery about it. I felt that there was a lot that I still hadn't come to grips with, and that there was plenty more to learn. I liked its mystery and its romance.

Just one last thing I'd like to say about Cuba. I was reminded of this when driving to the airport beside the beachfront. Mr Castro did something which every politician could learn from. One of the first things he did when he got into power was to build these huge play-grounds near the beaches, with slides and swings for the kiddies and all that. Of course, you're not going to say what a horrible bloke Mr Castro is after that. If I was a politician the first thing I'd do is to build huge playgrounds – nobody's going to say that's a bad idea, are they? I know people want schools and things but that's being like Father Christmas.

So you might well ask me if I'd ever be coming back to Cuba, and I'd answer you, 'Hmmm. Yes. If Mr Castro's got the time.'

Seville

Seville is Spain's fourth or maybe third largest city; has a population of 710,000 people, which is relatively small; and it's in Andalucía, which is the southern province of Spain, and quite close to north Africa. The thing about Spain is it's not a particularly populated place, and I think the less people there are in a country the less it changes.

Something I did notice about Seville, which is one of its charms, is that it's very clean, very tidy, and although this part of Spain isn't rich everybody looks very smart and they do seem to have a nice time. It really looks like it hasn't changed. It reminds me of when I was little: my grandmother and her brothers and sisters, they all used to come to Seville for their holidays and my Uncle Elbert (as it was pronounced – his name was Albert) would come home and he'd say, 'Gawd strewth, love-a-duck, it was ninety in the shade,' and I never knew what he meant. I never had the faintest idea but of course he meant ninety degrees. That's another thing, degrees are much better in Farenheit than centigrade because they're far more accurate; for example, the difference between ninety-one and ninety-two. I know that difference. Who changed that? And I won't give them an inch because if you give them an inch they'll take a kilometre. Anyway, they used to bring me back bullfighting posters that had my name on them, little gifts like that, and I know they used to come here and have very happy times. I've been looking round at some of the older people and they looked the same as my family would have seen then, they had ties on and little hats and things, and it was rather charming. I think the people of Seville are conservative and they don't like the place to look different. In fact, I think up until the First World War it hadn't changed for hundreds of years; it was pretty much like it had been since the fifteenth–sixteenth century when Columbus set off. And it's only this century that it's become a bit modern. Part of its charm is that it's slightly stuck in the fifties. And it's deliberate. It's not because they are kind of behind, it's because they think, This is quite nice, let's keep it like this, and I would agree with them.

One of the first things I did on coming to Seville was to meet up with Ana Corbero, an old friend, who'd agreed to act as my guide and translator. We met at this large cigar factory which once employed ten thousand people; I think it's supposed to be the biggest factory in Spain. It's a huge classical building and it looks like an old architectural drawing because the windows are blacked out. This is where the legend of Carmen originated. The story of Carmen is based on a girl who worked in the cigar factory whose boyfriend was a bit boring so she fell in love with somebody else. Then the boyfriend stabbed her.

We decided to start our tour of Seville in a traditional way … I was a bit worried about using a horse and carriage for transport because it's the sort of thing I would imagine Judith Chalmers doing in one of her travel shows – nothing against Judith Chalmers, but that's not the kind of vibe I was looking for: I was trying to chill out with the babes. But in the centre of Seville it's actually much quicker to get around by carriage because it can go where the cars can't. The cars have to go round the outside of town because the streets are too small.

It was interesting seeing that the coaches have leaf springs, and coach lamps of course, and they were coach-painted. Modern cars tend to be rather badly painted, with spray guns a lot of them, but coach-painting is where they paint it with a brush, flat it back with sandpaper then polish it with T-Cut, which makes it shine, then repeat the process. You keep doing that until you eventually build up this deep shine which is what coach paint is. It was a treat to see that; if you see an old steam lorry they have all been coach-painted.

So, Ana, Seville is the capital of the area of Andalucía. Is that right?

Yes.

Did I say that right?

You're making progress.

Thank you. Now. I'm enjoying learning Spanish and the pronunciation. So it's Andalutheea. Is that how to say it?

Yes. Andaluthía.

An-da-luth-í-a.

Th. Yes. Put your tongue underneath your teeth.

Andaluthía.

That's it. Well done.

It's a very old city, isn't it? Seville.

Very old. A little treatise was written about some remains that were found. It turns out that they were pre-Roman. And it was claimed that in Rome there are some sculptures, marble sculptures, of dancing women that actually have castanets and flouncy skirts.

So flouncy skirts and castanets predate Roman?

Yes. And the Caesars would send for these fabulous dancers.

From Seville, you mean?

Yes.

That would make it one of the oldest cities in Europe?

Yes. And also Hadrian came from here.

Hadrian of Hadrian's Wall?

Yes.

Generally the things that I look for in a city are a nice bar and a nice restaurant, I want a nice view, historic sites, maybe a bit of a knees-up and then to take in an art gallery. Because most cities of any size, even provincial towns in Britain, have very good art galleries. You don't have to know anything about art at all. Any sort of major town (you could be talking of maybe Leeds, Manchester, Seville, or Aberdeen even – you don't have to be in London, Paris, New York), they all have an art gallery and have interesting collections. A lot of them have the whole history of art in about three or four rooms. Hull is a very good example of that. If you go round the Hull City Art Gallery, for instance, you start off with two sort of fourteenth-century pictures, two sort of fifteenth. In a few rooms you reach the twentieth century and that's it. And it is great. You see a history of the world really. It's a treat.

Now in Seville they've got an amazing art gallery, Bellas Artes. It seemed to me there was no security or anything; they allowed us to set up and film in the courtyard without the usual problems. Their collection is largely Spanish art and I would say 80 per cent of the works there are religious. Sometimes it's better just to look at one or two pictures and leave rather than quicken your pace and try to run round the lot, and the picture I really would recommend anybody to see would be the one of the Eternal Father by Zurbarán.

The artist really has done a champion job because one look at it and you immediately know without even having to go up and read the inscription that it is God. And that really is good. It was like seeing a portrait of your own best friend, or pet, and immediately recognizing him (not that I ever knew God as a pet, of course). I put this to the test by asking each person who entered the room, 'Which one's God?' and they could point it out immediately. I think it's great because there aren't many programmes in which you can show Him. So that's been a nice advantage. A nice selling point for the show and I would like to thank Him for appearing.

It's quicker by carriage

And I would recommend going to see this other, Dutch picture in a different room. I don't know who it's by, but I'd been walking round the gallery and I'd seen lots of pictures of different saints, and martyrs, different pictures of the Crucifixion, of Christ being taken off the Cross, of them all weeping when he's being laid down and the adoration of the shepherds, endless religious pictures and eventually you get to this one picture of a Dutch garden. It's quite a relief because nobody is doing anything dramatic in it except picking a few apples or something and having a perfectly nice time of it.

The idea of visiting Seville came from going to a party that Ana threw to celebrate her first wedding anniversary in the small town of Carmona, which is about twenty miles from Seville. (I refuse to acknowledge such things as kilometres, litres: for me it's feet and inches all the way.) When we were in Carmona, which is a delightful historic hilltop town, I also had a day's visit to Seville which gave me the idea to come here. Also the music was great. At the anniversary party, after dinner this band slowly walked in, playing this rhythm; it was the local Carmona band, ordinary working musicians, not trying to be groovy or anything, just doing their daily job. Anyway, they came in and the rhythm they played (and this is what sent a shiver up my spine; this happens whenever anything sort of locks into place) was exactly the same rhythm that I hear in records like 'Iko Iko' from New Orleans or in Bo Diddley records like 'Hey Bo Diddley' or the Rolling Stones record (which they took from Bo Diddley) 'Not Fade Away'. As I say, I got this shiver up the back of my neck, the same as I always get when this sort of recognition occurs.

Earlier that day I'd read in my cheap guidebook (which the whole programme is based on, in the same way as every show we do) that Seville had been the first major trading port between Europe and America and, more importantly, the trade had been between Seville and New Orleans. Now they say in New Orleans that the rhythms come partly from the black slaves, partly from the martial, marching drums of both the British and the Spanish soldiers. Then the Creole thing makes up the sound that was to become jazz, which in turn was to become rhythm and blues, which in turn was to become rock and roll. So I suppose that shiver of recognition was because all of this had come out of this part of the world and from north Africa, because as I say we're very close to Africa here. I thought of people like Dr John and realized that some of his music sounded partly like Spanish soldiers playing, it's part of the rhythm of the jazz, and I'd never really taken it in until hearing it at this party. So that's why I wanted the Carmona band to come and play, to try to illustrate how their rhythm has been under-pinning pop music for years. The songs also are not dissimilar to a lot of blues songs. They're love stories where something's gone wrong or someone's been unfaithful. They are songs of the people and in a lot of places these days in the world it's the kind of folk music you'll find, like the old singers in the London pubs which disappeared years ago. It's like what would be considered a bit hokey; these people aren't from the big city, they're just doing what they like, and that's the appeal of it. The reason they do it is because they love it.

On top of that, they have a great charm and ambience about them, because they are up all the time, wanting to sing and dance – which is lucky as one of their jobs is to be booked for parties. They play a great deal so they're as good as professional musicians, but they've all got jobs in the day as well. They work in this little village, on the farms, whatever, and there's great honesty about their music, and it's alive. It's just them enjoying themselves and communicating that to the audience. In other words, once they start to perform they're having a party all the time. They include dancers and singers. They just love what they're doing and I think that comes across in the rhythm of the music, because it is really exciting and underpins popular music. You can't ask more than that, can you?

So anyway, I wanted to get them all together for the programme. However, after all that, the wrong band turned up.

The band that played at the party was the stand-in band for the band that came today. I was talking about this particular room from that night and they didn't know what I was talking about – there was just one man from the rhythm section of the large group that had played this thing, but that was all. Anyway, this is the *other* band from Carmona. But we still worked something out. Initially there was big stress because nobody knew what anybody was doing, but the great thing about music is that eventually you can understand through it. I didn't speak their language but Ana communicated for me. Actually, it's hard enough communicating with other musicians in English, because what one person will call a chorus another person will call a verse and vice versa. So for Ana (who is a great painter but not a musician) to try to explain what's going on was pretty tricky, but she did well. I was very pleased. Our styles are a million miles apart, but I got the excitement of their rhythm and we could play together in fifteen or twenty minutes.

The other *Carmona band*

I think that's what music is all about. In lots of ways it's a microcosm of what the world could be like if it were a little improved. This is true of any piece of music I've been involved in or worked on with anybody at any time, the whole point of all the great musicians I've ever worked with, everybody bows to the one god, which is the song or the piece of music you're playing, and anyone who is any good will not play at the time when it's not appropriate to play because what they are working towards is the benefit of the song. That's more important than any individual part and the Carmona band all did that.

Although a lot of people in England would think that bullfighting was cruel, the Spanish see it as being a sort of dance – a dance of death. And like a lot of blood sports it prepares people for their own mortality. They take the view that the thousands of creatures killed in abbatoirs every day stand no chance at all, but maybe some of the bulls do stand a bit of a chance, and at least they have a chance of participating in a noble ritual. This is their view; I'm not saying it's my view. I don't know if the bulls look at it like that but how do the bulls that are getting knocked into hamburgers every day in England or for our shoes and so forth look at it?

The people who attend the bullfights are incredibly well dressed; I hadn't realized that before. It's very, very popular. Teeming with people. They are all extremely well mannered and although it is not for the squeamish I could see how there's a theatre and a macabre beauty about it. I'll ask Ana to explain what she thinks about it all.

Basically, as you were saying, bullfighting is not about cruelty. It's a way of life, a kind of ecosystem. You know, if the bull has the freedoms that it has, in a way it has a much nicer life because it has this kind of sacrificial role in this society. So he is, in a way, a hero in the oldest sense of the term, i.e. the hero is the one that dies. So this animal which otherwise would be like any other animal that man has anything to do with – i.e. he would end up either as a piece of clothing or a plate of food – he is given an opportunity to (a) get the man; (b) have some dignity (it's not like going to an abattoir); and (c) save his life. Because, you know, if the bull is very, very brave the public will ask for his life to be spared. They are going to ask for his life to be spared because they think that courage and bravery are good, so in a way they are reinforcing the values that they would like to have. That's the kind of point the people who love bullfighting will make in defence. Another point that you didn't make but that I think is valid is that wild bulls were once common throughout Europe. They're a very, very old animal, and you find them in the frescoes in Crete, and the only place where they still exist is here. So otherwise they would just be vermin, if you see what I mean, or they would be completely domesticated and they wouldn't be wild bulls any more, they would just be cows.

Anyway, it was thrilling to join the well-dressed crowds and go through the sun-soaked streets of Seville on the back of a horse-drawn (coach-painted) wagon to the famous eighteenth-century bullring, *plaza de toros,* as they call it. Ana was explaining to me the theory of the . . . what is the name of the sleep they have in the afternoon? Oh yes, siesta. Which of course is not at all a sleep – a lot of the people have basically a naked cuddle-up or pleasure themselves or whatever they do, and *then* have a sleep. And then a lot of them will wake up and come to the bullfight which is at the right sort of time. So you have had life and death all on the same day. The theatre of life is played out before your very eyes. I quite like the love bit, and I've got an open mind about the death bit. I think any blood sports, whether you approve of them or not, certainly make you think of your own mortality.

I didn't realize how popular bullfighting was as a sport; there are some twenty-five thousand bulls killed every year, and 30 million people watch it every year, and the stars of the bullring – not the bulls, but the humans – can become millionaires because they're the great sports stars of Spain.

Los toros, as the Spanish refer to bullfighting, is a ritual that can be played out in two very different ways. The first is the more famous, and in it the protagonist is the matador, an individual man (or woman) who is aided in his battle by two mounted picadors and three banderilleros. An older, more aristocratic form of bullfighting involves fighting the bull from the back of a horse. The rejoneador, as this type of bullfighter is known, relies on his incredibly well-trained and brave horses.

According to Ana, bullfighting was always from a horse in the old days. In the eighteenth century it was just something that the nobility did, but there was this cheeky commoner who went and did it on foot and then it became a sensation.

When we met the great Antonio Vargas I noticed one thing: they say that every bullfighter is very sensitive to animals (although of course they have to dispatch a lot of them to their end). Sometimes they'll just look at a bull and they can tell, This is the one that's gonna get me, and yes, that will be the one that kills them. They can tell by just looking in its eyes before the fight. And the thing I noticed about Antonio V. is that he had perfect poise, like a dancer, and he had rather hard, not cruel, but hard, eyes. However, when he was with the horses that trained for the ring he spoke to them constantly. I was very impressed by this – he didn't stop once.

For the opening link of this film we did a trick where it appeared that I sat on a horse and then rode off. I was brought up in London and I'm more familiar with how to steal a Ford Cortina than how to ride a horse. I have great respect for those who have mastered the equestrian stuff. I enjoy looking at horses, and Antonio's horses were very beautiful. Then he very kindly lent me his horse. On film it looks like I ride off into the sunset, but then I step into camera shot so that it emerges that it isn't actually me charging off into the distance. But for a while I had to sit on this horse, which I did, heroically. But they were very good and he didn't let go of the horse once, I'm pleased to say.

When we interviewed Antonio it emerged that as well as the horses he has a model of a bull on a wheelbarrow to practise with, instead of a real bull. As Ana said, it looked like something a Spanish surrealist had made. During our film one of his men went into the field where Antonio trains horses and ran around with the wheelbarrow. Antonio ran around with the horse, and the man with the wheelbarrow looked like a bull chasing Antonio on the horse. Of course we got our cameraman chasing him around as well. The whole thing had a rather absurd look to it. In fact we couldn't help but laugh, and I fear Antonio may have taken this the wrong way, but it was no disrespect to him and his craft, it was more the absurdity of our cameraman, Eugene, running around after a man with a wheelbarrow shaped like a bull, who in turn was running after a man on a horse, and our soundman Tim, running behind him with a microphone. All in circles.

I did also say to Geoff that I thought it would be a good idea to have the wheelbarrow there when we interviewed Antonio, because I was going to ask him what his most terrifying moments in the ring had been (animals don't speak, so you can't ask them). According to Ana, he had had very many frightening moments. He told her that the most

I'm more familiar with a Ford Cortina than a horse

frightening moment was when he had a very bad accident and he was paraplegic for a while. So I thought that if the wheelbarrow had been there he could perhaps demonstrate the odd spill he'd had with a bull. But then I realized it was rather improper to ask that. When I mentioned the idea of having it in shot to Geoff he just said to me: 'Look, you've got the most beautiful creature in the world, this stallion horse, and this perfectly poised man, and you want to do the interview with a fucking wheelbarrow.'

If you have got to walk all day round these streets, it's very important to have the right footwear. I was in Holland once – and that's another thing, if I ever travel without a handkerchief I always regret it, I always get a runny nose and it's really annoying. So I always have a clean handkerchief, and I always wear sensible shoes. So, anyway, I was out in Holland and I didn't, I just had my plimsolls or something, some flimsy type of footwear. It was raining and we happened to pass a shoe shop, so I stopped the car and bought a pair of boots. These boots had written on the side of them 'Panama Jack', and the other people in the band noticed it and thought it rather amusing. But then later on we went on a walk across some dykes and stuff, and where they were sliding and falling on their faces in the mud, Panama Jack with his boots didn't slip once. I've had them ever since; they're absolutely maintenance-free and they've never let in a drop of water.

So this is why I held up the crew this morning, giving them a shine. I thought it was worth the delay because a very nice man offered to shine my shoes for what I calculated to be about eight pounds. A reasonable sum, I thought. At first I thought it came to about two quid. But we later calculated it to be eight quid, but as they are now like new it was well worth holding up the filming. When I told Ana about this bargain she looked surprised and told me the whole thing had cost me eighty pence.

*

I do like the Spanish temperament. Essentially I think it is very much like mine. I think I look a little Spanish and could blend in as one. To help this along I wanted to learn a few expressions in Spanish and I wasn't sure what to learn. Apparently Salvador Dalí could speak no English at all when he went to America and so he learnt only one expression, which was: 'It's not enough.' People would say to him, 'How's your hotel room?' 'It's not enough.' 'Are you enjoying America?' 'It's not enough.' 'Fee big enough?' 'It's not enough.' Whatever you asked him. 'Would you like to come out to dinner?' 'It's not enough.' So I've decided to learn that expression in Spanish, which is (and Ana had to teach me this) – '*No es suficiente.*' I've also learnt how to say 'big wanker'. I haven't used *no es suficiente* yet but I have used the other one with Geoff a couple of times. Ana, how do you say 'big wanker' again? I've forgotten already.

Gran hilipoas.

Gran hilipoas. When Salvador Dalí went to America, do you think it would have helped him as well as saying that's not enough if he had alternated it with wanker? I think it would have done, and why not have it at your disposal?

We were highly honoured to be invited by His Grace the Duke of Segorbe into his gardens. His family own a lot of big houses in France and at the beginning of the century the family had three hundred country houses. They are one of the oldest and grandest ducal families of Spain. The gardens are particularly amazing because there's the Moorish style crossed with the Roman style. Also the house is said in some ways to be like Pontius Pilate's house, which (it's claimed) the duke's ancestors visited. And there's a bust of Julius Caesar up on one wall which was done by somebody of his time – so it's a true likeness of Julius Caesar.

I was particularly thrilled by seeing a gigantic helmet and club which Ana directed me to. We wanted to film it or film by it. Before Geoff arrived I had a ten-quid bet with Ana that he would make the same joke that I had just made when he saw this great big giant hat and club.

He would say, 'Ooh er, see the size of those things, we better not be here when the bloke comes back to get them.' And he made exactly that joke and a very good joke it is. However, when we asked the duke about these objects he said, 'I'm not in the slightest bit interested.' He didn't know why everybody wanted to film and look at these giant things, there were much more interesting things to see there.

Then His Grace was kind enough to walk us through his gardens, pointing out the amazing tilework; at one point the family owned a tile factory so it was almost like a showroom. Also of interest were the beautiful fountains which the greatest musicians would tune to the right notes. So the fountains would be tuned in a musical manner. Something I'm going to engage in myself when I get back to London

Bring back the traffic!

in my own little windowbox. If I can just figure out how . . .

After leaving the palace we decided to slow down our pace even more by getting on a boat. It's a touristy thing to do but as Ana will tell us that's not a bad thing to be in Seville. In fact, when tourism came to the city visitors would go around saying: 'It's beautiful! How beautiful!', so they call tourists here 'the Beauties'. And indeed that's how we refer to our party.

I spent my first week looking at the Torre de Oro (Tower of Gold) labouring under the misconception that it was the tower belonging to Pedro the Cruel. I kept annoying Ana by referring to him as Pedro the Unpleasant. They also had other kings like Alfonso the Wise and so forth who were kind, so let's not tar them all with the same brush. Pedro the Cruel imprisoned Santa Ines, whom he had taken advantage of while she was tied up in his tower. She disfigured herself, because she was so beautiful, so that he wouldn't enjoy her company any more. Rather a horrific story – she poured boiling oil on her face. So here it is, this lovely tower that was covered in gold, with gold inside. All the gold of the Americas was stored here and it was covered in gold mosaic. Then it got ripped down. But somehow I was led to believe it belonged to Pedro the Cruel. Apparently it's nothing whatsoever to do with him.

Apart from looking at the tower, I learnt something from the boatman – the people in Seville are all very happy. He'd pointed out a bridge which some people were living rough under, and I asked if they were happy. He said, 'Yes, perfectly happy.' So that's good. And by the way, it's not only the people who are happy here in Seville. We saw some dancing dogs in the street when we were shooting round the town; this old man had some dogs that danced. They looked very happy. These little dogs were in flamenco dresses and Geoff seemed to be mystified by it all but I do think it improved the look of them.

To the Spanish people, flamenco is more than a dance – it is an artistic expression of the joys and sorrows of life. Its origins are Andalucían and it is traditionally performed by gypsies. In fact, Andalucía has Spain's highest percentage of gypsies (who are more integrated in Seville than in other Spanish cities). Famous flamenco dancer Manolo Marín has run a dance school for more than twenty-five years. There are about a hundred students, mostly from Spain, but also from the rest of the world. However, it is hard to learn if you are not Spanish, largely as its skills are a matter of individual interpretation. Students can learn the basic techniques in six months; but to be a truly accomplished flamenco dancer takes years.

Antonio Gaddes, the world famous flamenco dancer, told me the most important thing about dancing was the nose. How you carried your nose. Meaning you shouldn't be looking down, you shouldn't be looking sideways, you should be proudly looking ahead.

Everyone would think it's the hands or the feet or whatever, of course that's very important as well, but I am saying the key to flamenco is that attitude. I mean, it's about soul. If you've got the soul, the mojo, *then it's good. If you've got the technique and no* mojo *then it's bad. Somebody may be trying very hard to get at the 'Now you turn, now you …' Forget it because then you never get to the 'felt' bit.*

So, it's all from the soul and the nose.

My gypsy friends, they've just had two grandchildren and the grandchildren are one and two. They don't know how to talk but they are already going around clapping and singing out of tune and wiggling and they can't speak yet. Whenever they start doing it the whole family goes, 'Yes, yes', encouraging them. If you have that at three, by the age of nine you're laughing.

Manolo, as most great artists do, had a point. And his point was this. I asked him could anybody learn to dance and he said yes that they could. Anybody could learn the steps, most people could learn the technique and moves but (and this rang true with me as a person who plays a musical instrument) you really had to have a gift and have an instinctive ear for it. That is what the great dancers have and he could identify that in young dancers when they came in, when their faces lit up with the music. That, I suppose, was when he could see that they loved and instinctively understood their subject.

The guitars which accompany the flamenco dance were traditionally made in Seville. The best wood comes from the cypress trees, and Andalucía grows the best trees as the weather is very dry. Alberto Pantoja Martín is in his late sixties, and has been making guitars in his workshop in the Macarena district for the last thirty-five years.

The first thing I recall about his shop was the smell that you got of the wood and the glue. Then its black and white chequered floor and its wooden shelves filled with tools and saws and all sorts of things. It was really like a picture from an old Dutch painting of an interior with a man working in it. Drawers full of strings – it was lovely.

Now, the main difference between the classical and flamenco guitars is the latter has a much stronger body. It's built in a much more robust manner, because it gets knocked about a bit more. It takes Alberto two months to make a guitar and there's a year's waiting list. They cost about a thousand pounds, which isn't too bad.

His unusual pear-shaped guitars are the shape of the original guitar. He copied that, including the machine heads and the way the neck and the head are on the guitar, from paintings of the time (I suppose from the eighteenth century or before). In the nineteenth century, I think, a bloke came along (whom he mentioned – I can't remember his name) who invented a new guitar which the modern guitar takes its shape from. The larger soundbox gives it the more sonorous sound.

At one moment this professor came and played with Alberto. He's a professor of music and he was playing on a guitar which Alberto had made. Seemed rather a nice man. While we were waiting for the professor to tune up, Geoff and I managed to have a photograph taken of ourselves. Geoff likes to draw attention to himself, as he did here. He's

Overleaf: nine out of ten for the model village

often been photographed with celebrities. At one point he palmed himself off as the fourth Beatle. He had a T-shirt printed showing him actually hiding Ringo with his guitar.

I realized what a huge influence Spain has been on the world, especially the countries in the Americas, because of the Spanish trade. It must have been the most powerful nation in the world at one point, mustn't it? And the Spanish influence in the Caribbean is very strong. In Jamaica for example they would have had that cross between English folk songs, songs from the African slaves, and the Spanish conquest, and of course there are the Syrians and everything now. And let's not forget gypsy music comes from Spain. A huge influence on the world which is there all the time, a constant and popular culture.

A lot of people only know the macarena as a dance where people stick their arms out in the air in a line, and a lot of people associate it just with that dance but of course it's an area.

A feature of this area at Easter are these rather strangely dressed people, the Penitents. When you see pictures of all these processions it can look rather terrifying to the untrained eye, but they are simply repenting their sins and don't want to be seen, so they've got these hoods on, and it's nothing to do with the Klan. I don't know why the Ku Klux Klan have decided to use that as their get-up because it's nothing to do with them really. It's like any uniform, I suppose. Somebody told me that the swastika was originally a Hindu peace symbol, but the baddies always nick the best costumes, don't they?

The Macarena has its own joke attached to it. It is supposed to be an area of Seville where the people are very silly. I suppose it's like people used to tell Polish jokes or Irish jokes (but we don't want to get into offending anybody). So, this pianist from this Spanish area where people are reputed to be stupid goes into a concert hall, gives his concert. Everybody applauds madly. When he comes off somebody says, 'You're from this area of the stupids?' and he says, 'Yes, but how did you know?'

'Well most people go up and they pull the stool away from the piano and they then pull it up and sit down. You left the stool where it was and pushed the piano out and then pushed it back in again.'

EXPO '92 celebrated the five hundredth anniversary of Columbus's voyage to the New World. They held an Expo in Seville in 1929, which unfortunately coincided with the stock market crash. So it didn't really have the desired effect of drumming up trade. And then there was the one in 1992 which is interesting because it's 29 backwards – that's the only connection between them that I could see. They built this huge Expo site with various things, and most of them still remain in use.

I do enjoy a model village. There's a very nice one at Babbacombe, but the one in Seville that was built for the Expo outdid it, I was rather surprised to find. There's quite a nice one in Broadstairs as well – it outdid that one as well. There's a very poor one in Southport – the buildings just aren't realistic. I'd give the Spanish model a good nine out of ten actually. The only thing that might have improved it is if a miniature Foden lorry had towed me round on a great big raft in between the miniature buildings, but that's asking a bit much. That would have got it a ten.

The building which they put up for the 1929 Expo is incredible. It's made of brick, and it has two gigantic pavilions at each end which must be a hundred and fifty to two hundred feet high. It's very ornate, with arches and columns and colonnades – and that's just the two pavilions. On the building itself is a great arc with colonnades, fountains and statues and benches, and a lot of it is faced in terracotta. If you wanted to build one today I can't imagine what it would cost, millions and millions of pounds. It looks very much like a building of 1929 – rather gloomy and big. And built for nothing, really, just for show. Now it's government offices. There is another building built for the exhibition in the Moorish style, and it happens to be where some of the *Lawrence of Arabia* film was shot.

The old station, too, is in the Moorish Islamic style. It's quite weird because the body of the building is similar to King's Cross or somewhere like that, like you'd expect a station to be, but the detailing – the windows and the arches – is all Arabic, so it looks rather odd for some reason. I hadn't seen an Arab-style station before, so that was a treat. It has now been closed down because the spot where the lines ran out of the station was between the town and the site of the Expo, the world fair. People would come from town to get to the world fair, and would cross the railway tracks, and kept getting run over. So rather than put a fence up they thought it was easier just to close down the station and move it altogether, so they built a new one somewhere else.

Ana told me a very interesting thing about Seville Cathedral. During Easter they get these young boys to dance a minuet in the church in eighteenth-century costumes. This is the only church where there is dancing, but before the Pope had it banned you found it everywhere. The Pope tried to ban it outright. But here dancing and music is in the blood, and they didn't like that at all. So when they were told that they weren't allowed to dance any more, they said: 'Please, please, let us dance as we've just had these new costumes made.' I think it was a bare-faced lie. 'Can we at least dance until they fall off?' And the Pope said: 'Oh, all right.' So they proceeded to make these indestructible costumes which lasted for about three centuries. I think the ones they have now are new, but originally they would perform in these really old ones, costumes made out of metal. Anyway, the original costumes did finally fall to pieces, so they had to stop, except for the boys dancing. Probably by then it had become so entrenched – though now it's only ritualized. So it is just the boys doing it only the once at Easter time. They perform what is known as the *seises* which Ana explained to me means 'the sixes'. It's a traditional dance of Seville.

Filming with Vicente Amigo

The Giralda Tower was built in eleven-whatever-it-was. It was part of a mosque, but then the Catholics booted the Moors out. Then in Columbus's time, in the late 1400s, a huge cathedral was built on the side of this Moorish tower. In a lot of ways it sums up Seville. You have this Moorish Islamic style crossed with the Renaissance.

In the church itself, what is remarkable is the double organ – it must be nine storeys high. Walking around, you see the scale of the cathedral and the detail of the work. Also, you definitely get the idea of the magnificence of God, which is rather good because I think that was its intention, to impress upon the public the power and glory of God.

When they build churches it's nice to reflect the awesomeness of God in incredibly big and well-built things made by the greatest craftsmen. I think that's the best type of cathedral. We don't want anything too simple. Me personally, I don't mind a sort of simple mud-daub-and-wattle hut. But there's always a bit more to look at in a cathedral – if you are there during a rather dull sermon, there's always something to look at, isn't there?

On the last day we returned to the Duke of Segorbe's gardens, which, as I said, have a strange mix of Moorish and Italian architecture with all these sculptures bought back from Naples in the sixteenth century by his ancestors. We filmed in there with Vicente Amigo – an incredible guitarist. A lot of guitarists are brilliant with their left hand but only play one note at a time with a plectrum with their right hand. Vicente uses all the fingers of his right hand and plucks the guitar like that, which is quite amazing. I didn't realise just how good he was. I've heard his CDs but when he plays in person he is even better: the sound and the precision and the beauty of his playing.

He was keen for us to try to do something together as well as performing on his own, and we tried a piece he'd written and (although the chords and harmony are pretty much the same, well, they are the same wherever you go) the time signatures are very unusual and so you are never quite sure whether something's a waltz or in 6/8 time or 4/4 time. But after playing this piece through a few times something seemed to come of it which I was really pleased with, which was great as music is an international language. He didn't speak a word of English, and apart from the phrases that Ana had taught me – *'no es suficiente, el gran hilipoas'* – I spoke no Spanish. None of these was appropriate to use while working with him when we'd only just met. So it was only music we had to communicate with. By the end of it, for me, it worked. It was a fantastic place to do it in and sort of magical, because before we began one number the bells of the local church were ringing. Then all these birds started to sing as well. In fact one of these tiny little birds did a crap which landed on his jacket, which as we know in England is a portent of incredible good luck. I always remember when I was about twelve and staying with some friends of my parents, I went out on a very sunny morning in a nice convertible car and a seagull crapped on my head and I was told how lucky I would be – and I was. I managed to get this translated for Vicente and he seemed to be very amused by it. He laughed a great deal.

I also had a chance to look at some sculpture in the garden. The duke had shown us around some of it but I hadn't really taken much of it in. As well as there being a contemporary bust of Caesar, there was also a very sexually explicit picture of Leda and the swan, where the swan is having sex with her. Zeus is disguising himself as a swan so that he can get saucy with the ladies. Normally this is depicted with a swan on a lake and Leda looking at him; you have to guess the rest. But this one has graphic detail of the swan mounting Leda, with her giving him a hand, I thought, and loving every minute of it. The other thing that I spotted there was the sleeping Venus, which came from Naples. I've never really studied sculpture before properly, although my wife, Christabel, is a very noted sculptress and I look at her work all the time. This incredible sleeping Venus or Sleeping Beauty (I'm not sure but it didn't matter that I didn't know) was so perfectly formed and the same size as a human. First of all I put my hand on top of her hand and that was lifesize. Then I started to feel the curves of the marble, and that was a private moment – there was no one in the gardens. One of the great things about sculptures is touching them, which is of course not what you are meant to do in museums, and I started to feel the curves of her body and she was perfect. All of us have an idea of what the perfect shape might be and she seemed to be it. I felt underneath and all her back and her bottom felt perfectly curved as well and then I felt compelled to kiss her gently on the lips, which is what I did. Perhaps I'd been overcome by the music of Vicente or just tired because we'd been working for a long time. Then I also looked at her profile, close up as you would to a loved one, and I thought it was so beautiful. I put my fingers over her lips and nose. I noticed her elbows and her arms, and how beautifully formed they were. Geoff then dragged me off and the co-author of this book comforted me and I was led away. But what I'm trying to express is that I think I understood entirely the intention of the artist and what a fantastic craftsman he must have been. I have great respect for artists and craftsmen, which I suppose Vicente is as well. Not only can you have the idea to do something but you can physically make it as well. Out of what was of block of marble, you can create the perfect human form that you just want to stroke and take home and pet.

Beirut

I first heard about Beirut from Miles Copeland, who used to be my manager, and managed Squeeze and the Police. He'd been brought up in Beirut because his father was important in the CIA there. Miles Copeland and his brothers, Stewart, who was in the group the Police, and Ian, who is an agent, went to the American college in Beirut. His mother was an archaeologist and she found some of the most important missing parts of the Dead Sea Scrolls, the translation of which she thought was actually going to change the way the Jewish people thought about everything. She said, 'They're so important I'm going to hand them straight over to the national museum.' However, Miles Copeland Senior said, 'You can't just hand them over – you must document them first.' So he took them on to the roof of their house in Beirut and photographed them, at which point they just crumbled and disinte-grated in the sunshine because they'd been underground for five thousand years or something, and so now nobody knows what they bloody said.

I knew that there were lots of biblical references to the Lebanon, and I'd been told that most of the references occur in the Book of Ezekiel. Now this was of particular interest to me as there is this church in Deptford (St Nicholas's Church) which has two flaming skulls on the gateway which terrify most of the people who visit it. I was told that this was from the story of Ezekiel.

I like to be prepared, so I thought I'd better reread the Book of Ezekiel. Of course my own personal family Bible is a very large, embossed, illustrated, Victorian one. We were going to Salisbury the weekend before my travels to do a show, and I had to bring it along in the car. It was, after all, a Sunday. At the time my brother was away, so we had Mick Talbot, who among other things was half of the Style Council, playing with us instead. When he saw me struggling towards the car with this huge book, and then saw me with it on my knees throughout the whole journey, I could tell he was pleased that my Bible studies were continuing. Maybe he hoped we could share moments from the good book together. Unfortunately I was unable to take it with me to the Lebanon because of its size.

I got through part of Ezekiel that day but didn't discover any hard facts about Lebanon itself. However, I did know that it is always referred to in the Bible as 'the land of milk and honey' and it's mentioned in the Song of Songs, and I believe it's where the water-into-wine incident happened – well, it is of course just around the corner from where everything was going on then.

When I was on the plane there, I read that one of their greetings translated very similarly to the Geordie expression 'All the best to you and yourn for the coming twelve-month,' which I'd heard in the north-east. I thought, Well, if that's their type of attitude in Beirut, I want to get to know them. I'd heard that the people were friendly, and in fact it was supposed to be, or had been for years, the most fun place of the Arab world and the Middle East.

The population is between 3 and 4 million but nobody's quite sure because they don't want to do a census, as it might show that there are more Christians or fewer Christians or more Muslims or fewer Muslims than they thought, which would upset everybody.

It's a long narrow country on the edge of the Mediterranean. It is only about 30 miles across, and about 150 miles long. From the sea it goes straight up into two huge great mountain ranges, and I think the geology and the shape of the country have dictated a lot of its history. The currency is the Lebanese pound; at the time of travelling there were 2400 Lebanese pounds to the English pound, which meant that a tin of Coca-Cola was in excess of four thousand quid.

I'd read that since the war finished in 1992 it really wasn't too dangerous. On the drive from the airport to the centre of Beirut I saw that there were soldiers at checkpoints everywhere, but they all seemed quite courteous. The army or the police have checkpoints scattered throughout the city, but on the whole you just have to slow down as you

Where's the hubbly-bubbly, Walid?

approach them, show that you're willing to stop – and then they wave you on. This is unless they think you have an especially sinister look, I suppose. Sara, the producer, told me that Geoff had already been pulled over by the police once before I arrived. Of course he didn't have his papers with him but luckily managed to get out of it. And of course as soon as the police had got their backs turned he said things like: 'If one of them says the wrong thing I'm gonna flatten him.' I'm sure he didn't mean it in the slightest.

Anyway, peace, no matter how fragile it is, has reigned here for the last six years. Although it's been a turbulent country for the last ten thousand.

There used to be a group in London called Walid Joumblatt and the Druze Militiamen, so I was glad that our first interview was to be with Walid Joumblatt himself. Mr Joumblatt is the leader of the mysterious Druze sect. The Druze people originally lived in the mountains, and they were landlords and warlords. Somebody told me they are famous for having the most polished manners, but it is also said of the Druze that you can go to dinner with them but you mustn't sleep in their houses. This expression apparently comes from a time in the middle of the last century, when they said to some of their enemies: 'Let's make peace and we'll have a huge banquet for you.' So they invited them all round, and had this huge banquet, and fed them and entertained them, had special tents laid on for their guests of honour – and then murdered them in the middle of the night, slit their throats. Just like the massacre at Glencoe in Scotland, I suppose.

I am assured that Joumblatt's father was a very spiritual man, who used to meditate all day long and things like this, but I had no idea what sort of person Walid was going to be. However, I got an indication when I saw his large villa with two armed security men, and inside a number of Range-Rovers and a huge new white Mercedes 500 long-wheel-based vehicle. The window was half wound down on this Mercedes, and I was very impressed to see that the glass in it was about an inch and a half thick. Oops, I thought, we'd better be careful.

The modern Mercedes, which we see quite a lot of in Beirut, the Mercedes S600 limousine, would cost you about £75,000 to £80,000 in London. Apparently they only cost $40,000 here which is why every Tom, Dick and Harry's got one.

We were taken to the first floor, a large room. I was interested to see there were sort of Charles Eames chairs mixed with the odd Arabic painting and it was a general mix of I would have said of . . . not aristocratic taste . . . more International Smart Person's taste. The look of someone well-to-do.

He had large eyes, a moustache and was bald and rather tall. He was also, I wouldn't say grumpy, but concise, let's say. However, he did have this lovely smile – when he smiled he really put you in good humour. Everything sort of cheered up. But when he didn't smile it was really not so jolly. And when he smiled again, it was as if the sun suddenly shone from behind the clouds.

He told me that he thought the current Prime Minister, Rafiq Hariri, had ruined Beirut because he had flattened what was left of the old town and was now putting an entirely new city in its place. Furthermore, he said, 'I don't like modern Beirut, it's no good.' I asked, 'Why do you live in it?' and he said, 'Well, I have to. Business connections and that.' And of course he's the leader of the Druze so where else would he go?

Finally I said, 'Any message for the Prime Minister?' I can't remember exactly what he said, but it was something in the region of 'Just tell him he's ruined the place. What can you say to a fool?' So, as you can see, he was quite outspoken. However, I didn't mind him, in spite of his rather curt (I won't say unfriendly) manner.

Also he's known for smoking a hubbly-bubbly pipe. We didn't see him smoking his hubbly-bubbly, unfortunately, but we *were* offered Lebanese coffee when we were there, which is very strong. Rather like taking sulphuric acid and crack cocaine together.

We went down to the market which was inhabited largely by Palestinians. It was a poor area and it reminded me a bit of Brick Lane in London. However, unlike Brick Lane, there is still terrible evidence of war damage – this area is known as 'the belt of misery'. A big building which had been a hospital during the war was now a home for displaced persons. There were large areas of bombed wasteland and the buildings were shaky and bullet-ridden.

There were cages full of chickens and as soon as we pointed the camera in their direction a man obligingly whipped one out and offered to slit its throat for us, which he then did, even though we didn't ask him to. That's the freshest sort of chicken, let's face it.

There were stalls selling electrical goods, fruit and vegetables, and it had the hubbub of an old Arab market. There was a man selling hubbly-bubbly pipes and we bought one for $20. It was marked as costing £30,000 Lebanese pounds, that is. I really like paying for things with Lebanese pounds because it makes you feel very rich, spending £30,000 on a hubbly-bubbly pipe. I told the man that I was going to give it to my mother, but I don't think he really understood that.

I'd experimented the night before with this sort of pipe. They put a little bit of tobacco and then a kind of honey in it, and it burns for up to a day if you have a person stoking it up for you, and you just inhale the whole thing through the bubbles; it's like a mild cigarette. Geoff had to carry this large pipe down the street and he said: 'I don't know if I should carry this, it makes me look like a bit of a wanker.' But, as Eugene the cameraman helpfully pointed out, 'You don't need that to look like a wanker.'

Another man came up to us at the end of the shooting and presented me with a great big lighter. I thought he was trying to sell it to me but he wasn't at all – he was saying, 'No, please have this as a gift, it is so nice for us that people are coming to film here.' Geoff thought it was probably a bomb. I've got it in my bag and it hasn't gone off yet.

After a rather long Japanese lunch in our air-conditioned hotel, we set off on a long drive through the vicious heat in our non air-conditioned bus. We were heading to the Jeita Grottoes to film the famous Lebanese violinist Nida'a Abu Mrad.

The grottoes at Jeita are one of the natural wonders of the world. They are millions of years old and were discovered in the last century. They consist of a series of large underground caverns with huge stalactites and stalagmites. I had never seen anything like it, though I have been to Peter Pan's Pool at Southport, and the Chislehurst Caves, and Cheddar Gorge.

Nida'a Abu Mrad then told me, at *great length*, the story behind his music. He's a Sufi, which means a mystic really, and so his music was based on this. It is part improvisation and also played on a completely different scale to Western music. It looks at things from a mystical perspective, from both the Muslim and the Christian sides. And he wants to be a conduit for God to play through him, even just for a moment. It was fascinating, although, as I say, a little long – I've shortened it for the benefit of the reader.

The inside of the caves apparently goes on for about five miles but they are lit for only half a mile, which is as far as the public can go. Anyway we set off on these launches and it was like being in an Indiana Jones film or maybe *Journey to the Centre of the Earth*. Eventually we got to a room that was enormous – it must have been about 150 feet high, like St Paul's Cathedral – with these gigantic stalactites and stalagmites littered all over the place; some have taken hundreds of years to form, and some have taken millions.

I went to and fro in this boat several times, and each time saw something different in the rock formations. Sometimes I saw people's faces or an alien's legs, the Leaning Tower of Pisa, or a silly dog with a large ear over one eye. If, like me, you can easily see a fish's face in the bark of a tree-trunk the Jeita Grottoes hold unlimited visual treats. I said to Geoff that it was like a giant ink blot – the sort psychiatrists give psychopaths to find out about their characters. He said that if a

psychopath was brought here he'd probably go mad with overload.

It was one of the most magnificent works of nature I have ever seen, and great that we were able to have this man filmed there, playing his mystical violin, trying to work with nature and music and all that. Overall it was an incredible spectacle. The girl, one of the two accompanying singers, had a marvellous singing voice as well. When the violin stopped and she began to sing you couldn't tell the join between the two – a complete naturalness that I don't think I've heard for a long time. Also the acoustics were like those in a cathedral.

The only reason we were able to film there was because the Minister of Culture approved it as a cultural thing; if we'd wanted to film a travel show or a commercial video they wouldn't have let us do it. (Nida'a Abu Mrad does the occasional concert in these grottoes.)

The curator of the caves, who was trying to be helpful, had a Bobby Charlton haircut and a beard and was looking rather worried and nervous about everything. He said that he'd gone into business with the government. In other words, he'd taken a franchise out on the caves. Once we'd filmed the people on the boat, we wanted to film someone just looking up at these incredible sights. He suddenly started shouting: 'You can't do that! You can't do that! You can't start filming the stalactites and the rock formation – that wasn't part of the agreement!' I think the problem was that the inside of these caves is kept completely secret. They are open to the public but you're not allowed to take any photographs or film there. He feels that if it is revealed on film, no one will want to go.

My main reason for coming to Beirut was my friend who lives and works here, Nabil Gholan. He's thirty-six and quite a successful architect. He also happens to be married to my old friend Ana, who was our guide in Seville. He's a very clear-thinking man and talking to him had convinced me that Beirut would be an interesting place to come to.

Nabila Metwally and the international language of her body

The second evening, he came round and collected us in his Range-Rover and took us for a tour of the city. He started by pointing out the tallest building in Beirut. In the war, he said, it had been used as a sniper's hide-out because you could see almost anywhere in Beirut from it. After the war it was discovered that the rooms had been cemented up and they'd just had little holes so that the snipers could point at a particular street. There were certain streets you couldn't walk down because the snipers' guns were pointed at them. It also overlooked the main highway that goes from east to west Beirut, part of which is a tunnel, and it was impossible to use that highway then. People who drove through often got shot as they came out, and then you couldn't recover the bodies for days. Anybody trying to get close to them would be shot as well.

We then drove around to what is called the Green Line, which divided east and west Beirut. It was called green because it was made up of shrubs and plants. Nobody would cross this open area, it was virtually deserted; and because of the weather conditions all sorts of trees and vegetation sprang up in no time whatsoever. So it was literally a green line going across the city. And in the buildings either side of it the people would be battling it out. The fronts of the buildings facing on to the Green Line would be completely riddled with bullet holes and mortar holes and everything, whereas if you went round to the back they would all be like new, untouched, because people were all firing from one direction.

In other parts of town he showed us where aircraft had bombed buildings, and it's quite strange to see a block of flats with six or seven floors on one side of it all leaning down like vents on an air-conditioning unit. He also showed us the Hilton Hotel, which had just been built and was about to open when the war broke out, so that it was never occupied. Then he drove us round the centre of old Beirut, where there's this huge development going on. Out of a population of 3 or 4 million people, I think there must be a million people working here – it's extraordinary how fast they're building. But because there's been a city here for so many thousands of years, there're ruins everywhere you go, so as soon as you start to excavate, putting the foundations for a new skyscraper, you stumble across a great work of Roman or Phoenician antiquity. A lot of the time everybody just stays stum and builds on top of it anyway, because otherwise you couldn't build anything here – it would all be one giant archaeological site.

From Nabil's apartment block you could see a little quarter which is what the whole of Beirut used to be like: little streets, old houses, restaurants and shops. He said that this was the only bit of old Beirut left; everything else is modern as it has had to be rebuilt. You could see what a real blow to a city it is when an old part of town is flattened; the whole character of the city changes.

This left us all feeling a little sad, and in Nabil's case a little nostalgic, so to cheer everyone up I told a joke that Geoff had told me earlier (and had repeated many times): A bear goes into a bar and says, 'I'll have a light ale and … um … a packet of crisps, please.' The barman serves him and says, 'But why the big pause?'

Roderick and Mary Cochrane live in a house that his English family have had for years, called the Palace of Sursock. It was quite extraordinary, a villa surrounded by maybe three or four acres of land, and once behind its walls, trees and hedges you could no longer see Beirut. You could be out in a posh villa in the country. The house was in the Beiruti style, but it felt like an Italian villa.

In the garden we filmed Nabila Metwally, the great belly dancer (or rather 'oriental dancer', which is what they are called). The night before, we went to see her performing in a restaurant. She had explained to us that her body is like an international language, because when she's dancing she listens to the words of the song and interprets those words, whatever they are, so that everyone can understand them. She was very graceful and her body could move in incredible ways. She'd been dancing since she was a small child.

Nabila, in fact, reminded me that Salome's dance for King Herod happened not far from here: a man being seduced into submission by the power of this dance. So much so that he cut off John the Baptist's head. This is the power that these dancers have, because they can hypnotize you with the movement of their body, and persuade you to do just about anything. Geoff certainly seemed to be putty in her hands. However, she was there with her husband (who was also her manager), who seemed a rather world-weary man. I suspect he was probably very worried that he might lose her because she was so beautiful.

We decided to have a musical experiment because I wanted to see if I could fuse the blues with some Arab rhythms. We got three Arab percussion players, and I played the piano. The song I played was 'Reconsider Baby', a Lowel Fulson song that my orchestra once did with Eric Clapton. Nabila danced to interpret the song. It's an experiment that I've never seen done before, mixing blues with Arab music and then having a dancer interpret the words, and I think it was very worthwhile.

For our transport here we wanted to get a jeep, but we couldn't locate one, so we ended up with a Swinging Sixties bright red Mini convertible. There are a number of things about driving here that you have to understand before you set off. Firstly, they have hardly any traffic lights, so at every junction people just slow down (fractionally), and then weave in and out of one another's way in order to get across. There's lots of people beeping, but the tooting of horns isn't done in an aggressive way ever, it's always 'Look out, I'm coming through here.' So on all the roads there are lots of people giving way and waving and they somehow manage to make it work. There are also no drink-driving laws and until a few years ago there were no MoTs or driving licences even. I asked people how they got a driving licence, and they said they were given them as presents or perhaps just bought them.

We were stopped by the army when I was with Nabil and they said: 'Let us see your documents,' and he simply seemed to get out the service history of his Range-Rover to show to them. Which seemed to satisfy them perfectly, so on we went.

After the Second World War they brought in a French (which seems a bit odd) motoring expert who advised them on how they could make the city's roads run better. After much studying of these roads he said, 'It works perfectly well, I can't understand why it works, or how it works, but somehow it just does.'

With very old stories, there are often conflicting views of what happened and where, but there is quite a strong tradition that the story of George and the dragon took place here in Beirut. We filmed by the very old cathedral of St George, which was built by the Christians during the Roman Empire. A version of the story which I discovered here, and that I'd like to share with my readers, is as follows:

The King of Beirut was being menaced by a dragon, which had come right to the edge of the city wall. So, each day, the town worthies would just drag out the nearest person and sacrifice them to the dragon. The King realized that this was causing general panic among the populace of Beirut, so they all agreed they'd better get democratic and start drawing lots to see who'd do it. Of course, as these stories go, the first person who was chosen through drawing lots was the King's daughter, the beautiful princess. And to show that he was a man of integrity, the King agreed to let her go. So she was sent out and left for the dragon to gobble up. While she was there busily praying to God to be saved (because she was a Christian, of course), along rides a Roman soldier – our George – who sees her, and asks her what the problem is. And so she tells him, and they end up both sitting there, praying together. At which point the dragon turns up, and George gives it a complete pasting. One of its more unpleasant habits is breathing poisonous gases which choke and kill people. But he either (according to some versions) bit it, or (as other people say) he got it right in the neck with his sword, which stopped the poisonous gases coming out, then spanked it about, and said: 'You're not doing this any more!', and dragged it back to the city. Yet it wasn't quite killed, and everybody said: 'Will you please kill the dragon? You've done really well but could you just kill it now?' He said he would if they all converted to Christianity. Which they immediately agreed to do. And the King was so pleased that he handed George half of his gold and valuables, which George then distributed among the poor of the city. Then of course he rode off to England and converted us to Christianity there. And then he became the patron saint of England.

We were taken to a site where this was supposed to have happened, and where a mosque has now been built, but it was really just a pre-fab behind a petrol station. So I prefer to think it was more likely to have taken place at this large Roman cathedral.

We also drove past the great mound of old rubbish that's called the Hill That Farts, because of all the methane gas produced within the bowels of this revolting pile. It literally farts at Beirut every once in a while. I won't make any comment on this – I think we'll move on to graver issues.

I was very impressed that the research team managed to secure an interview with the Prime Minister, unlike our failure with Mr Castro.

I was shown into the residence of Rafiq Hariri, and there he was, reading a newspaper in his study, which was decorated with the *Encyclopedia Britannica*, and Lebanese books. He had a short-wave radio in there, and lots of pictures of his family being given doctorates and things like that, wearing mortarboards.

He is quite interesting because he was originally the son of quite a poor man – well, I don't know if he was poor exactly, but he wasn't somebody involved in politics or powerful in any way. Most of the people involved in politics here come from political families. Which is why Walid Joumblatt said, 'Oh, but he has no culture.' Mr Hariri went to Saudi Arabia, and made a fortune in building projects. He then came back to Beirut to become the Prime Minister in 1992.

The Lebanese are very clever like that. Merchants. The Phoenicians invented the alphabet, so first of all they are very literary; but they are also people who have enjoyed the deal since classical times. I think that quality is perhaps what the people like about Hariri.

Another thing they like about him (and he was elected with a reasonable majority, I believe) is that they think he's probably not as corruptible as a lot of other politicians. He's not going to take bribes because he just doesn't need the money. He has been seen to put millions of his own money into hospitals and things like this.

The Prime Minister was very genial and he talked to us at some length. He did make one unfortunate language slip, when we asked him about the plans for rebuilding central Beirut, and about how they'd started. He answered, 'I first decided that I wanted to interfere.' And he paused and said, 'No. *Interest* is the word that I mean. I first took an *interest*.' But it was very nice of him to have us there.

I regret not asking Mr Hariri to comment on Walid Joumblatt's rather rude remarks about his rebuilding of Beirut, but one of the things I have learnt in television is that you can't ask all the questions that people suggest. I think the Prime Minister would have laughed and risen above it though. One of the questions I should have asked Mr Joumblatt was 'Did you know there was a group in England called Walid Joumblatt and the Druze Militiamen?' But I didn't really like to. I didn't want to lose that lovely smile.

While I was there, the British Ambassador arrived and said a quick hello to us. Then he took Mr Hariri to one side, and they began sharing jokes and chatting earnestly about things.

I rather hoped that we'd see a Rolls-Royce Phantom II limousine dating from about 1965 waiting for our ambassador outside Mr Hariri's house as we left. And maybe a liveried footman. I wasn't far wrong – there *was* a Rolls-Royce Phantom II, but sadly it wasn't the ambassador's. He had a very smart white Land-Rover, with what I would describe as two very useful SAS men with machine-guns standing around it. One of them said hello to me. And I thought, This is proper British security. And the car had a Union Jack on it. My heart leapt with a little beat of pride.

On the outskirts of Beirut, by one of the large military bases, there is a huge monument which is seven storeys high. It resembles a very thin block of flats, and it's completely filled with old tanks. It's a work of art called 'A Monument to Peace', by the French artist Armand Fernandes. It was put up after the war finished in 1992, and there was a plan to put it in the centre of town. However, the residents of Beirut didn't want that, because they really would rather forget about the war and having to see tanks every day. Instead it has been put up outside this military base, and it was sort of impressive to see. To be honest, I don't think I would have wanted it in my garden, though.

David Maclennan (the British Ambassador), me, Rafiq Hariri
(the Prime Minister), Geoff and Eugene O'Connor

While we were filming this, the people from the military base had to check our papers and that took quite a while. While this was going on Geoff started to expand on a particular conspiracy theory which I hadn't heard before. Here it is (and again I must emphasize that it's *Geoff's* theory; I don't want Glenn Miller's family to sue me): Glenn Miller was not a band leader and was not killed in a plane crash going from England to France as was believed. According to Geoff, he was shot in a French brothel in the middle of an assignation by the gun-runners whom he was involved with.

Now I said to Geoff that I thought it was quite possible that he wasn't killed in a plane crash. And I had heard that perhaps he had died in the arms of a woman in France. But that's rumour, and really who can tell? But as for his being a gun-runner … I said, 'Well, it seems unlikely to me, Geoff, that Glenn Miller, who was a very successful musician at the time, would have wanted, or needed even, to go into gun-running.' Geoff said, 'No – he was forced into it by the Nazis.' So I said to Geoff, 'Well … why was he taking guns to France, which the Nazis had occupied for quite a while. They could have just sent them up in lorries. Why did they need to be smuggled in his trombone case?' At which point he seemed to lose his temper and started facetiously saying, 'And Duke Ellington never played the piano, he had someone sitting behind him and putting his hands out of his sleeves.' I think the heat had got to him. But that's how we stood, beneath the Monument to Peace, arguing about Glenn Miller and gun-running.

To change the mood slightly, we went on to the Riviera Beach Club on the Corniche. From the very name of the place you could tell what it was going to be like: glamorous, executive-lifestyle, with packets of Rothmans and dimmer switches. And indeed there were lots of suntanned, movie-type people sitting around under parasols, sipping Martini's wearing flimsy bikinis. I, on the other hand, was very nobly wearing my heavy black suit and shoes, for continuity purposes, and sweating profusely as I walked with my heavy Gladstone bag. A few of them looked up – and I think I heard just one or two remarks as I went past, and they were giggling. I could hear Geoff muttering, 'We're English, we're English.'

At the Riviera we were met by a very helpful friend of Nabil and Ana, who took us out on his boat so we could film the coast of Beirut. We filmed people swimming in the sea and having a perfectly nice time of it, and young lads diving off Pigeon Rock. I believe there is a tale that heart broken people have a habit of going to the very top of it and throwing themselves off, which is rather sad, when you dwell on it. It was very beautiful and picturesque.

Back on the Corniche, we met up with one of Beirut's great actresses, Nidal Ashkar. She told us what life had been like before and after the war, and how she thought that the one unifying thing of the Lebanese character was that they were very determined people. So no matter whether they were Christian or Muslim or Druze or whoever it was, after the war they didn't wait for the government to help them, they just rebuilt their own houses, did whatever they had to do. I must say, I began to think that she was a fine example of their determined character.

She also thought it was very important to build up the culture of the Lebanon: a lot of that has gone, because of the war, so the young have no idea of their own identity. Then a very young person, about seven years old, crashed into her on his bicycle. I said perhaps it would be good also to bring cycling proficiency tests in. She agreed with me very forcefully.

While we were mingling with the beautiful people of Beirut at the Riviera Club, we were delighted to spot a friendly face: it was Dalida, one of the girls from the Four Cats, Lebanon's newest girl group sensation. They are Lebanon's equivalent to the Spice Girls, I suppose. Anyway, Dalida was wearing a very charming Union Jack bikini and seemed quite pleased to see us. Earlier we had filmed them all, in the Sursock gardens. They are very popular in Lebanon and were number one in the charts when we filmed them. Dalida had been a contestant in Miss Universe, Zaina had been a weather girl for the Future TV channel and Chantal had been Miss Elegance last year. There had been another one called Rula, whom I'd been told was studying architecture. (It's quite a good name for an architectural student. It's a bit like if your name was Thomas Square: you'd be T. Square, architect.) But just as I'd asked her, 'Now what about your architectural studies then, Rula?', the others said, 'No, it's not Rula. We got rid of her – we've got Nicole now because she's a model.'

They were lots of fun and very positive, and we wish them a lot of success, as every country needs its young pop idols. Upon reflection, I think I could share the following opinion with my readers with a certain confidence. In the same way that probably the best cigars come from Havana, the best wine comes from certain valleys in France, and the best diamonds from certain mines in Africa, I've got the feeling that the best young pop groups probably come from Britain. But it's nice to see other people have a go at it. It really is.

On Monday things started very early. We all climbed into the bus, and I should point out what a friendly man that bus driver was. He was probably the most good-humoured member of our party during this early morning ride. It was quite a bumpy journey, with people having stayed up late the night before, and not feeling their best, so it was an unusually silent one. Indeed, I think Geoff probably had two hours' sleep the whole time he was in Beirut.

Anyway, we arrived at Byblos, which really is an incredible place. Dr Helen Sader, who is a top archaeologist in the Lebanon, was waiting for us. She was very illuminating. Very concise and fascinating to talk to. Byblos is as impressive as the Seven Wonders of the World, she explained, but nobody really started to excavate the site until the 1920s. A Frenchman began it, and he had three hundred men working for him. She said this was really unfortunate: as he was the only archaeologist, and the three hundred men digging were just workmen, the work happened much faster than he was able to keep a record of. So they just dug and dug and dug, and found all sorts of things, a lot of which weren't recorded. Apparently the Frenchman took a lot of things home, and seemed to give a lot of things to the man in the restaurant next door, Pepe. The notes he did manage to make were all scribbled in pencil (and they're in Geneva now anyway). When I said that it wasn't a very helpful thing for the Frenchman to have done (I couldn't help saying, 'Typical ...') the point was made quite strongly that our very own Lawrence of Arabia had managed to put quite a lot of ancient Syria in

The Four Cats

his pockets. He brought it home, and gave it away to friends, and some bits to the Ashmolean Museum in Oxford, and the British Museum in London, and kept choice bits for himself. So the French archaeologist was clearly following a great and honoured tradition here, and not simply being light-fingered, as some might think.

Then we ran through the history of Byblos itself. There is only one reference work, which is written by this Frenchman. They discovered that there had been a city on the site of Byblos for around ten thousand years. It is an idyllic position, because it is on the sea and below the mountains. First was a Neolithic settlement; I guess a village of mud huts and that sort of thing. (And you can just imagine what was happening in Blackheath at that time. I suppose it must have been a big swamp. We must have been about two foot tall back then, and not even living in caves, I would imagine.) The Phoenicians were next and built a proper city there, in about 4000 or 3000 BC. They built a huge city with temples, and their kings were buried in great sarcophagi. (I've heard all this rubbish about five hundred people in Hertfordshire trying to build a pyramid. When they couldn't do it, they said it would have been impossible for anyone to have done so in ancient times, so the Egyptians must have had help from astronauts. I don't think it was that, myself. I think they're just very clever at carrying things in this part of the world. In Beirut I happened to have a piano delivered, with two men carrying it. As a professional pianist I've had all sorts of pianos delivered in all sorts of ways, but I've never seen a piano carried by two men in such a way before. It was brilliant and simple, and with sort of straps around their necks. My readers can refer to the little sketch which I've very helpfully made of their method of lifting it. It was incredible. I thought, Well, these people are obviously very advanced at knowing how to carry and move things around. Which is why they were able to build these great things. But I digress.) The sarcophagi, had the earliest form of alphabet written on them, and so I asked Dr Sader what the first letters said. She said it was written that a curse would be put upon anybody who dug them up or disturbed the remains inside. I said, 'Oh, that would be the French-man, Monsieur Twatter – what happened to him?' She didn't know. But I would like to find out whether he (or his children, or his children's children) has been cursed. I would be very interested to know.

I also noticed a set of obelisks laid out three in a row, with one slightly to one side. There's an identical formation of giant standing stones at the side of the A1, the Great North Road in England. I'm sure they all add up and form a link across the world, but I really couldn't bother myself with how or why.

After the Phoenicians came the Romans, who arrived just before the birth of Christ and left about three hundred years after his death. It was a period when they were all rather relaxed, not so warlike. One of the things I was really excited to see was the Roman nymph sanctuary. The columns have all fallen over, and the capitals are all lying around, so it looks like a large theatre set. But you could still make out the base of the sanctuary. I'm not exactly sure what its purpose was. I looked up 'nymph' in my dictionary and it said that it was a young goddess, a sexually promiscuous young woman, and also an immature insect. But, looking at its size (it must have been about sixty feet across and the columns were about fifty feet tall), I don't think this particular nymph sanctuary was created for young insects. And I can't imagine how it would have helped sexually promiscuous people particularly, because it would have all been a bit out in the open for them. So I think it was there as a sanctuary for the young goddesses, and it made me wish for some modern cranes (or a couple of old Lebanese lifters) to reconstruct the nymph sanctuary in my garden in Greenwich. I would spend the odd afternoon in it, like a spider in his web, waiting to attract the nymphs, and I would then spend many happy hours nymphing.

After the Romans left, the Crusaders came, and immediately knocked down a lot of the Roman buildings. They saw these buildings that were temples to this, or temples to that, nymph sanctuaries etc., and they just pushed them over because they couldn't care less, really. Then they built a great big ruddy castle over the whole thing. So in the centre of Byblos there was this huge Crusaders' castle and even now there's a little village around it.

What I really enjoyed about the site was that you could just go in, that there was no one looking over you, no bossy custodians like at Stonehenge. There were some lovely pots there as well which were from 2000 BC, in which they fetched the water for the temples. They were almost perfectly preserved, and bearing in mind that they were over four thousand years old I did wonder if the Millennium Dome could be made of similar material; then it might survive longer than the ten minutes it's currently supposed to last.

Next door there's the modern village of Byblos, with Pepe's restaurant where we all had lunch. It is famed as the best fish restaurant in the Lebanon – if not the whole of the Mediterranean. We sat on a lovely terrace and had lunch, which consisted of chicken and meat kebabs. Which we'd had every day. I've no complaints – we all enjoyed our lunch very much. But I think it might have been good if someone had had the foresight to order some of this famous fish. We didn't have any fish at all. We did have some chips though.

Pepe is now ninety, and he was what I can only describe as an Anthony Quinn European Character. I could imagine driving a sports car in the 1960s, and him being 'my old friend Pepe', that sort of thing. Anyway, he had his own small private museum at the back of his restaurant. In it he had the most incredible collection of Roman and Phoenician artefacts – indeed more antiquities than I've ever seen in a restaurant. Even better, in fact, than some of the greatest museums in the world. He says that he found them while fishing, just dived and got them out of the sea. He also mentioned that the French archaeologist stayed with him for quite a long time, and would give him the odd piece that he himself didn't happen to want. Some people rather unkindly suggested that during the war, when the place wasn't really looked after, he went and helped himself to whatever he fancied, and had a good dig around. But, having met Pepe, I can't believe that could be true.

In one of these ancient pots I noticed some twentieth-century litter. This was a good sign, I thought. If this site had been in England you wouldn't have been able to get within a stone's throw of it. You would have had to peer over the wall with a periscope, and there would have been guards, and if you'd tried to step anywhere near it in order to dispose of your rubbish, you'd have been immediately wrestled to the floor and ejected.

Some of the really delicate things have been put in the museum here (but the most valuable stuff, I think, was in Pepe's back room). If it was somewhere else in the world it would *all* be off in some air-proof room in a museum or something, but in Byblos it's all just there in front of you.

We had asked some folk dancers, in traditional costume with traditional instruments, to do a traditional dance known as the *dabke* in the amphitheatre there. One thing I've noticed on my travels is that folk dancing is remarkably similar throughout the world. Hopping from one foot to the other.

There was one thing about the place that gave me pause, and I'll reluctantly mention it again. The curse of Byblos. There's no question about it – you did feel, looking at the tombs of the Phoenician pharaohs and kings and whatnot, as though there was some presence. When I got caught short, I did try to pick a wall that looked like it had been a dull, mundane guardhouse to piss against, rather than somebody important's tomb or something like that.

Anyway, all in all, I left Byblos really very impressed because there is no other city that has been consistently inhabited by humans for ten thousand years, that I know of. After having had a rummage round that morning I made a point of washing my hands. After scrambling round a

Club BO18: Serge Gainsbourg raised a laugh

place that has had ten thousand years of constant human habitation
you do feel a bit mucky, especially with all the curses floating around.

As we left Byblos there were some fishermen repairing a boat, singing a
fisherman's song. I wondered if they were singing 'Zagwill', the oldest
song in the world, which is said to be still going strong all over the
Mediterranean. The chorus translates as:

> Laugh while ye may, keep toil and trouble at bay,
> Soon the dark night of death comes and takes us away.

And that's the oldest song known to man. I have the sheet music –
I think seventy years is the copyright so it's probably safe to use by now.

As well as having traditional Lebanese music and Arabic music in
general, we wanted to try to find out what their contemporary musicians
were doing. There is this group called Soap Kills, and one of their tracks is

The dabke – *or, hopping from one foot to the other*

'Salopette'. There was some confusion about what this word means. We thought it meant 'slut', but it might mean 'suspender belt'. Sara the producer, in a moment of over-eagerness, turned to the armed guard with us and shouted, 'Salopette!' at him in a bid to find out its meaning. And I must say he looked very confused; personally, I think it means 'slut'.

The club where we filmed Soap Kills was interesting. It has an odd name: BO18. It was in an underground room, and surrounding it was a sort of concrete area. You had to go down a metal staircase to enter the club, which was about fifteen to twenty feet high, about forty-five feet wide, and maybe a hundred feet long. The crowning glory of it was that the whole roof area had great hydraulic jacks and opened right up to the sky. On a very hot evening the whole roof could be opened up so the club would in effect be open-aired.

There was a small dance floor at one end and the rest of the floor was covered in small coffee tables made of solid marble, surrounded by low benches. On the top of these tables were placed – and fixed hard – photographs of some of the late, great musicians of the world. In front of each photograph was a little pot with a flower in it. So when you sat down, it was like sitting in front of shrines to some of the great musicians. They had, for instance, a picture of Django Reinhardt on one, Charlie Mingus was another one, Count Basie another, a few Arab musicians whom I wasn't familiar with, and so forth.

Although it's rather a nice idea to have a shrine to all these musicians I also thought, It's all very well, but then people just sit round and put their drinks and maybe even their feet on them. Also, as they didn't have names on the photographs, unless you were really a music-head you might not have known who they were. I sat quietly at the one of Count Basie, because I'd always liked him, and got rather annoyed at all those noisy, shouty people surrounding me trying to set up the shot. One of Walid Joumblatt's coffees would have gone down a treat as well just then; it had been a long day.

One of the last things we filmed was Mr Nadim Karam and his 'Archaic Procession', which is a collection of large sculptures. These are placed in what was the old part of Beirut, which is now completely flat, so it's like a large sort of square. He's made these large, rather jolly figures which, as you can see, dominate the square. I talked to the artist, who told me that they were always on the move. I asked him whether he meant if you had your back turned to them they'd move. He said rather sarcastically that he didn't mean that at all, he meant that they were on display in Prague one minute and another city the next. He had hoped to take them to London but he had an argument with the people in the Serpentine Gallery so they weren't after all going there. I shouldn't think they'd fit anyway.

Our plan was to go up in a cable car, but this was closed when we got there. However, on top of this mountain was a Catholic cathedral with a vast statue of Our Lady of Lebanon, which you can climb up to and which affords incredible views down on to Beirut. Next to it is a Maronite cathedral. There are seventeen official religions in the Lebanon. All the Christian ones, different Muslim ones, and not to forget all the sects. And they do (apart from the war of course) sort of get on, and have learnt to get on over the thousands of years of all being here together. There is such a long list of what all the religions are, really, and you couldn't simply mention the Shi'ites and the Druze and the Maronites because the names all sound nice when you say them, you've got to include the rest as well. And it's the same in their government. They have to have a Christian president, a Muslim prime minister, a Shi'ite minister of this, a Druze minister of that, to balance it up. So really we must say them all and I did so for the programme. I left none of them out. We don't want to start another war, do we?

It's also on that hill that I retold the legend of Adonis, which Dr Sader told me, because from there you can see the mountainside (directly above Byblos) where the story is meant to have taken place. I have often heard the word 'Adonis', because people sometimes whisper it as I go

'Our Lady of Lebanon' and the wrap shot in front of the 'Archaic Procession'

past, so I always took it to mean 'a regular bloke'. But of course it means 'great handsome person'. Adonis was the result of the union between a goddess and her father. The story is that she got her father drunk, and had sex with him, and became pregnant with Adonis. She feared that her father was going to come and kill her because of what she'd done, and begged one of the gods to turn her into a tree. Of that tree Adonis was born. He was so beautiful as a baby that first of all he was given to Aphrodite to look after. She fell madly in love with him, and wanted to keep him. In the end Zeus had to intervene. He told her that she could be his mother for four months, but that the rest of the time Adonis could choose where he wanted to go. Anyway, he then lived in the hills above Byblos, and Aphrodite came down from heaven to live with him. Despite a couple of bad omens (there are different versions as to what these omens were), he went out hunting in the woods, where he was gnawed in the groin by a wild boar. Aphrodite heard his screams and came running – but it was too late and he died. She sobbed and sobbed and sobbed as his blood ran out. It apparently ran down into the stream that goes out into the sea near Byblos. At a certain time of the year it goes red, and this is supposed to be Adonis' blood.

It had an enormous following, the cult of Adonis. They would have huge processions up into the mountains, chanting a thousand times: 'Oh, Adonis is dead! Adonis is dead!' And then they'd chant a thousand times: 'Adonis is risen! Adonis is risen!' and whip themselves up into a hypnotic frenzy. Adonis, of course, represented the rebirth of nature each spring.

And the women had to choose between shaving their heads or prostituting themselves to foreigners and strangers for this one day of the year, giving the money they made in this way to the Temple of Adonis. Of course, this became quite well known throughout the Mediterranean. People would know what the day was and whip down there. The whole city would become a sort of brothel for the day (apart from the women with shaved heads). Then about two or three hundred years after Christ the Christians thought, Well, this is just getting a bit out of hand now. So they smashed all the temples up, and stopped it all, and carried on with their more enlightened ways.

Finally, as a sort of souvenir, I would like to share with the readers Geoff's Beiruti joke. He was constantly telling it to people in Beirut, although I'm not sure how many people understood it.

A Beiruti man gets a job as a centre-forward for Sunderland Football Club and he's on the phone to his mother and he says: 'Mother, I've just scored a hat-trick for Sunderland. It's the greatest day of my life.' She said, 'Well, you should know, son, that the tanks have just rolled up outside the house, there's been some gunfire and our flat has been destroyed and your father's been killed.' 'Oh, Mother,' he says, 'how can this happen to me on my greatest day? When the first and the second goal went in the whole crowd stood up and were cheering – and it was just for me, Mother. Oh, how sad this should happen on this day! This is the greatest day of my life!' She said, 'Well, I'm very sorry to tell you this, my son, but also there was a sniper firing from across the road and your sister has got two bullets in the head. And she has been killed.' He said, 'Oh no! Mother! On the greatest day of my life, this has to happen! The whole crowd were shouting my name on the third goal, and they carried me shoulder-high through the streets.' His mother said, 'Well look, son, I'm sorry, but I never wanted to move to Sunderland in the first place.'

Dublin

My trip to Dublin didn't start off very well, because I almost missed the last plane there. The thing you find when travelling is that people try to hurry you along all the time. Boss you about, even if there's not necessarily a big panic. If you're the last passenger for a plane and it comes over the Tannoy, 'Will Mr X *please* board the plane,' don't run, take your time. There's nothing more degrading than to rush on, all out of breath, with half your clothes hanging off, to be booed by the other passengers for holding them up. It's best just to walk on in a dignified manner, and ignore everybody. Never panic at any time. If I'm in a taxi and I'm late for a plane, I don't tell the taxi driver to step on it. There's never any point in getting stressed. If you miss the plane, just get another one.

I was once in Switzerland, where the trains leave at *precisely* the time they say they are going to; when the minute hand hits the 32 at 11.32 it leaves, with or without you. I didn't quite have my bags on at departure time and a *very* bossy guard came up and screamed at me to hurry up.

Because he was screaming, all these memories of the war came back, and I put down my bags, half off and half on the train so it couldn't go anywhere, and said, 'I'm sorry, we're not going anywhere until you start being nice.'

I think all of us have some responsibility to stand up to these little Hitlers. If you don't stand up to them when they're little like that, they soon grow all out of proportion and they'll be the station master before you know it. And that would be no good at all.

By and large, it's easier travelling with a film crew than with a band. Maybe this is because the locals think you might be a news crew reporting on how annoying airport officials are. Musicians get an especially hard time, they always seem to be suspected – we've got a Rastafarian in our band and he gets stopped and searched every time, no matter what country we're flying to. So it might be as well to pretend you're a film crew even if you're not. Purpose of visit? Making a documentary about petty officials.

Anyway, I know that the Irish are famously relaxed about these matters, and as the plane was half empty there was hardly anyone to boo me. I prefer not to have to talk to anyone during these flights anyway; in fact I have made it more or less a rule never, under any circumstances, to speak to strangers. Something I was taught as a child that has stood me in good stead ever since.

A friend told me about this trick to use if it looks like conversation is inevitable: think of yourself as a spy, and you've got to discover every-thing about this person you're sitting next to. The first few times I did this I think I might have come across as being really rude, quite boring and rather unpleasantly nosy – 'Oh, how many brothers and sisters have you got?' 'Oh, I see, and what did your father do? Where did you live and exactly how much do you earn now?' etc., etc. Either you'll discover a great many facts about this person, or they'll make their excuses and move. It's all right doing this inside airports, but it's much riskier if you're on a plane. There's a danger that you'll be stuck sitting next to somebody who'll want to chat back and answer all the questions. All in all, I'd say it's best to keep coldly aloof from all fellow-passengers, even your own travelling companions.

Dublin is now one of the most visited cities in Europe, but I advise avoiding it at the weekends because it is so busy with visitors from overseas getting drunk. In the week it is a delightful place to be: the crowds are a bit thinner and there are some fantastic things to see. I make regular visits to Dublin. We play in the Olympia Theatre and the crowds are some of the best you could ever hope for: enthusiastic, dancing, having a nice time.

The city was originally built around the part of the River Liffey where there were some black pools; in ancient Irish, 'black' is *dubh* and 'pool' is *linn*, so: 'Dubhlinn'. Had they stuck with the English translation it would have been called Blackpool.

The entire population of Ireland is just over 5 million – that's including Northern Ireland. Half a million live in Dublin, and another million live in the suburbs, so clearly a large percentage of the country's population lives in the capital.

Although Ireland is an ancient place, originally inhabited by giants and fairies (much like England used to be), Dublin itself is a relatively modern city because it was founded in 988. This means that it's already had its millennium celebrations – in 1988. The Romans never came to Ireland: they got as far as the Welsh mountains and couldn't face going any further. The Spanish were a little cleverer, because they sailed round it. In some parts of Ireland there are people who look very Spanish because of these settlers; and the Irish-Spanish people are absolutely beautiful.

If you're looking up at the buildings to examine the architecture, you keep bumping into these little public sculptures that they have all around the town. There's one of Anna Liffia – she's supposed to personify the spirit of the River Liffey. Because she sits in this sort of shower which washes over her shoulders, she's known as the 'floozy in the jacuzzi' or the 'whore in the sewer' (it has to be pronounced 'whooer' to rhyme; an Irish accent also helps for the general feel of the thing). Then there's another one of Molly Malone, who we've all sung about in that cockles-and-mussels song. Her statue is known as 'the tart with the cart'. Finally there's one called 'Meeting Place' by a sculptress called Jenny McKenna. It's of two ladies sitting on a park bench with their shopping beside them. This is known as 'the hags with the bags'.

The eighteenth-century architecture is delightful in itself to look at, and there's a lot of history that goes along with it. There's an archway at Trinity College, beneath the belltower, and it's rumoured that if a virgin walks through it all the bells of the university will ring simultaneously. The bells have not rung for 270 years. I don't know what that says about the population or the students, or even me, as I went through it several times to test it.

As we were going around the market Geoff suggested that I buy some flowers as if I were a regular marketgoer. So I went along with this, then I realized there was no point to it at all except to look a bit sad, so I decided to give them to somebody as quickly as possible. I remembered this very nice old woman in the market who had told me that I danced like John Travolta. Now I do occasionally dance on stage but do it very seldom, and I don't think she'd been to see me perform. However, I thought it was very astute of her to know this particular fact about me. I went back and handed her the flowers but she said, 'You should give them to your mother.' I said, 'Well, I can't, because my mother's in England and the flowers will be dead by the time I get back,' which she thought was the funniest thing she'd ever heard.

Dublin, of course, is incredibly important musically. It's like New Orleans, in that musicians have gathered here for hundreds of years. The roots of rock and roll go back to Celtic music; not only did the Spanish bring their rhythms to Dublin, but also Celtic folk music was taken to America with the first immigrants. And of course more of them set off from Ireland to go to America than from anywhere.

One take of Van Morrison – the right take
Paddy Maloney of the Chieftans

It goes like this: hillbilly music in America came from the roots of Irish music, and without mixing hillbilly music and the blues you wouldn't have had rockabilly and rock and roll, and all of that. So Dublin is a crucial stepping-stone in the history of modern music.

While we were there we wanted to talk to one of the greatest Irish musicians: Van Morrison. He spends a lot of time in Dublin (although he's originally from Belfast). He bridges everything musically, and is the epitome of soul-meeting-folk music. We also wanted to film the Chieftains, because they have a certain way of mixing all that music together too.

I was delighted that Van agreed to come and do something in this film because he's one of the most important figures in music. Van said that when he was young Dublin was *the* glamorous place you headed for because it was the capital city. He said you could always have a good time in Dublin – but actually you could have a good time anywhere in Ireland because it's that sort of place. It's always a pleasure to be in a place like that – unlike, say, Switzerland.

I'd worked with Van a while ago and had been incredibly impressed. He only does one take of anything and that's always the right take. In that way he's like some of the great blues players from fifty years ago. He told me he wanted to achieve that again, and we were going to have to get it right straight away. He decided on 'Shenandoah', a song he recorded with the Chieftains for a documentary about the first Irish immigrants to America. As Van explains, it is like a gospel song, the sort he first heard Paul Robeson doing.

Van and the Chieftains performed this beautiful traditional song, 'Shenandoah', in one take. It worked very well – a perfect choice of song and especially moving in the ancient setting of the thirteenth-century Drimnagh Castle.

Paddy Maloney of the Chieftains told me about growing up learning music from his grandparents in the country, where everyone would get together for reel dancing and hoolies. He learnt from this traditional style of playing when staying with them, and then picked up the newer styles and influences back in his native Dublin.

In 1958 Desmond Guinness started the Irish Georgian Society, to preserve buildings that were due to be demolished to make way for new developments. Nowadays people almost go too far in the preservation of things, but in 1958 people were prepared to demolish whole crescents of delightful buildings and put up supermarkets. He wanted to show me a specific building he was interested in, and he chose the Rotunda Hospital, which has been a maternity hospital since the eighteenth century. In fact, Bono from U2 was born there. I'm trying to blend the buildings in with a bit of rock and roll history, just to give the readers a mixed cultural lesson. Phil Lynott, for instance, came from Dublin and he filmed a video in one of the Georgian archways.

The Rotunda's exterior is made of stone, and Desmond explained to me that the most important buildings in Dublin are made of stone and the slightly less important are made of red brick. They contrast rather well. He also explained why Dublin is now one of the most beautiful cities in Europe: it was preserved, in his words, by a 'cocoon of poverty' in the nineteenth century. The rich people moved out of the city and there was no money to redevelop it. So you now have these long vistas of red-brick, background architecture, and then you have the great stone fanfares, such as the hospital.

Next he showed me the chapel attached to the hospital, which is one of the most extraordinary and one of the least-known interiors in the whole of Dublin. It dates from the original building of 1751 and was decorated a couple of years later by an Italian stuccador. It must have cost a fortune. How could they justify spending all that money when the very poor were having their babies all around in the wards? He thought the reason was that it was actually a good investment. One of the best ways of raising money in the eighteenth century was a nice long tear-jerking charity sermon. But there's no point in having a charity sermon,

however moving, unless you have the place full of people with fat purses. Accordingly, they spent a great deal of money making this the prettiest chapel in Dublin, so as to attract the rich folk who liked pleasant surroundings.

One of the best and quickest ways to discover what a foreign city is all about is by asking taxi drivers. Dublin taxi drivers gather at the Café No Name, so that's where we went to meet them and have a chat.

They all seemed to think Dublin was much better than it used to be in many ways, and a lot of people are now coming to live and work here. There are lots of Yanks coming over here, making flashy films with big celebrity actors, so this was quite exciting. One of the lads had had Julia Roberts in the back of his taxi and had taken her to an exclusive restaurant for dinner. Another had had Alan Rickman in his – now he's a *proper* actor, you know, not like some of those Americans who just mouth the words. And he's British. And you could see when the taxi drivers said his name, they were all quite impressed, because after all he is one of the greatest actors of all time, probably.

Lots of people from the world of music and even the world of sport, like Damon Hill, have come to live here too. The Rolling Stones are in and out. A lot of people live in Ireland because of its ambience, but also because you don't have to pay anything like as much income tax. This latter was a brilliant idea by the Irish government. In order to have an affluent place, you've got to have affluent people. By making it easy for people from overseas to come and live here, just like Switzerland, the idea was that you could turn it around economically. It worked, and Dublin is fast becoming rather glamorous. In fact the area just outside the city where a lot of the well-to-do and the famous live, tax exiles and artists and whatnot, is known as the 'rockbroker belt'. Which puts it very nicely, I think.

My understanding (although it would be wise for readers to confirm this with an accountant) is that artists don't have to pay tax. Nor do non-residents. And Dublin is of course their first choice of city, because it's the closest thing to being back in mainland Britain – and that's what any sensible person would want, isn't it? (John Betjeman made this same point very beautifully in his book on the cities of England. He says that you can keep your orange groves of Italy, and your vineyards of France, because he's too busy being moist-eyed and nostalgic when he thinks of somewhere like Wolverhampton. I could say the same about Newark, in Cambridgeshire, where I went recently. One of the most delightful places I've ever been.)

They also told me that you get a lot of foreign tourists visiting Dublin, but a lot of these are Americans who have come to discover their roots. This also happens in England and Scotland. If asked, the majority of Americans will tell you, Oh, I'm an Irish-American, I'm an Italian-American, I'm a German-American.' And they come back to their beginnings in Dublin or London they always seem to need a few drinks. And the thing I can't help noticing is that instantly they turn into blubbering Irishmen singing Irish songs. Or if they're in London they're sobbing and singing 'Maybe It's Because I'm A Londoner'. And if, over seven generations ago, they had some uncle or cousin that once came from Scotland, they start wearing the kilt.

One of the hardest choices I have to make when I arrive in a foreign town is which method of transport I shall use. You've got to bear in mind that to some people this would just be a decision about transport: to me it's a way of life. I spend the greater part of my life touring so it's very important to select a car (or van) that is enjoyable to be in, and be part of, and that you can have some pride in. There are all sorts of different reasons for being attracted to a motor vehicle. The sheer engineering and Germanic reliability of a big Mercedes can be attractive for a longish journey, but likewise the well-made elegance of an old Rolls-Royce can be equally charming. We are also very dependent upon what is available from the local hire companies or specialist hire people; and it helps if you've got an open-topped vehicle so you can both film out of it and directly into it. I have always been very taken with the Rolls-Royce Phantom II; I happen to have a model of one.

Now you can see that this remains one of the most elegant cars in the world, even though it's bigger than a Transit van, with this enormously long wheelbase. But it's still one of the most elegant and well-built cars of all time. We tried to get one in Dublin, and unfortunately we couldn't, so instead we got another kind of Rolls-Royce (which is, I think, is a 20hp). But it's still a nice car and ran like a sewing-machine.

I had asked the taxi drivers who or what they liked to listen to while driving round the city at all hours, and they told me that what they most enjoyed was listening to the live arguments on the Eamon Dunphy show. They referred to him as a 'regular boy', whatever that means. The other thing they liked was the fact that he seems to enjoy it most when people disagree with him. He even reads out the bad messages they send him live on air; things like 'Eamon's a gobshite.'

Now, Eamon Dunphy is not only a radio talk-show host: he is a retired professional footballer who has written a book on U2. And now he has this talk show where people ring up and have rows on air. I've never seen the point of those types of shows. People argue enough at home. But now you also have to ring up the radio and do it publicly.

I was really looking forward to meeting up with him. I interviewed him in the back of the Rolls, which is an interview technique I very much enjoy, as you can view the scenery at the same time.

Eamon had some interesting views that I'm not sure I would want to argue with. He hated *Riverdance*, thought it diminished Irish culture, that it was a slap in the face to any genuine Dubliner. (I didn't tell him – I didn't want to start up an argument on camera in the back of our car – but my children really enjoyed the show.) He thought it was one of many bogus forms of Irish culture being sold to the world. He included Mary Robinson and Seamus Heaney in this general round-up. His country had

Interviews in Dublin were conducted in style
Eamon Dunphy takes his seat

given these things to the world, but it was only fair, because the world had forced all sorts of corporate things on to Ireland like the Hard Rock Café and McDonald's. So the Irish could be said just to be getting their own back for all these terrible inflictions on their native culture.

He called the Dubliners 'Dubs', which I thought was quite a good word for them. He shared my impression that they have this particular sense of humour which you don't get in any other city in the world – I can think of a few extremely humour*less* places but I won't name them for fear of giving unnecessary offence. Eamon reasoned that it's down to their having absorbed the best of all their conquerors before getting rid of them. And this is certainly a nice way to see it, and probably accurate. The other distinctive trait Eamon has noticed about Dubs is the incredible degree of literacy which the ordinary people have. If you meet a bloke walking down the street – a bus driver or someone cleaning the streets even – he'll have a huge vocabulary. More than that, they're very familiar with poetry, and novels and stories.

We discussed another very Dub characteristic, one I particularly enjoy. Most everybody here in Ireland has kept up with traditional music, and most everybody also has their own song, which they sing at parties. I explained to him that in England the old habit of families going out together with everyone singing round the piano in the pubs has vanished now. In Ireland it kept going, because the musicians still play in pubs – although I understood from Eamon that his children don't have their own songs, so maybe his was the last generation to continue this custom.

I blame a lot of its disappearance on the breweries: putting jukeboxes in pubs and taking the pianos out. And it has much to do with television of course; family nights out and sing-songs at the pub aren't very attractive to the television generation – although obviously I appear on the television sometimes myself so I can't knock it too much. However, I think it would benefit Britain if television closed down for a couple of years, and then maybe people would chat to one another and so forth, and play cards, stuff like that. Maybe even go to the pub and sing their own songs. Only then would I bring back television, but very slowly, and I'd be sure at the same time to ban newspapers, so they couldn't try to say awful things about the great success we'd had by closing down television in the first place.

To his credit, Geoff seems to have many songs that are 'his' songs, which he makes his own. He sang 'Danny Boy' quite a few times. I suppose 'Danny Boy', to a lot of Irish people, is similar to 'Maybe It's Because I'm A Londoner' – but it's far more important. It's one of the most beautiful songs of all time and each person who sings it makes it his own. Everybody from Mahalia Jackson to Ben Webster to the Beatles, you name it, they've done it, and it's been done beautifully. However, even 'Danny Boy' can get a bit tiresome when it's sung *all* night long. By the end of our stay in Dublin, after Geoff's relentless singing, I came round to the idea that television was probably rather a good thing.

Eamon did have some good things to say about Dublin. For example, he mentioned the recent achievements of the people from this city – 'right across the spine of popular culture' was the way he put it: Neil Jordan and Jim Sheridan's films, Brian Friel's plays, stuff like that. People are rightly proud of this. And Dubliners deal with celebrity with a healthy scepticism. So when Jim Sheridan came home with his Oscar they told him, 'Don't get too big for your boots, Jim, don't forget where you come from.'

I first met Mary Coughlan when she appeared on a programme I was doing called *The Happening*. I immediately warmed to her character and her voice with its silky tone – it really is remarkable. She's one of the greatest singers of all time, and she just gets better and better. There's something about the spirit of natural musicians that I particularly like. You can rehearse and rehearse and rehearse, but there are certain people who just do the one take and it sounds great. And Mary's one of them, like Van Morrison. She did the song 'I Want To Be Seduced'. In this case it was Geoff's brilliant idea to do that particular song. She'd recorded it once before but I think it sounded even better when we did it, I really do. And there was a tremendous look of pride on Geoff's face when it worked so well – he was clapping like an ecstatic seal. (The thing about Geoff is that he's so relaxed, and because of this he makes the whole thing go smoothly. If you've got somebody being all tense and precious in charge of filming, things just don't work as well. You've got to relax and let things flow.)

Afterwards we wandered down the famous Grafton Street, which Van sings about so beautifully in 'Irish Heartbeat'. Mary was originally from Galway but lives in Dublin now, so I asked her what she liked about Dubliners. She said it's that they're so opinionated, with absolutely no basis. 'For example, if you get in a taxi, the taxi driver starts talking to you like he knows everything about everything, whereas in fact he knows nothing about nothing.' I happen to agree with her that this is a very nice characteristic to have. A lot of my friends are like that. I hope I'm like that myself.

Geoff: 'You are.'

Two contrasting sets of buildings that represent the spirit of Dublin would be the Casino in Marino, and the Ballymun Estate. The Casino in Marino is a large pavilion built by William Chambers for Lord Charlemont in the eighteenth century. The main house has since been destroyed, and the pavilion is now surrounded by suburbs. From the outside, you notice immediately that there is this absolutely giant window on each wall, so that the building appears to contain only one large room. Once inside you see there are actually fourteen small rooms, each one perfectly decorated. It is the sort of thing you want to put somewhere you like, and have friends round for a knees-up.

The Ballymun Estate, on the other hand, was put up by the Dublin Corporation in the 1960s as a quick and easy way of housing lots of people. They seemed to forget to put gardens in for everybody, and the general view is that it has been a bit of a disaster. While I was there, the sun was sinking and the shadows were long, which gave it a rather surrealist look. It looked like a de Chirico painting. I don't want to get too tricky for my readers here, but if they could picture these huge grey slabs of buildings with the inhabitants and all of the animals running around, and then just very long green grass, and long shadows. It had a very eerie atmosphere. A lot of the young children there had squatted (with the help of their parents) in what was a derelict working men's club. They turned it into stables, and they race the horses around the council estate – there are children of all ages involved, and it's simply great. It gives them something to do, and keeps them out of trouble, and it's very odd to see these huge teams of people riding around through the great shadows of this estate. It's going to be pulled down, I believe, in the year 2000, and they're going to construct houses with gardens. I'm sure

The Ballymun estate

once it has finally gone people will say: 'Oh, it's all very well, but wasn't it great when we had those blocks of flats with horses living in them?'

We met Father Sean Breen, who used to work on the estate and also happens to own a racehorse. He told me that it is important for him to be very moderate in his gambling. Moderation is the key to everything, which I'm sure he's right about. He even repeated this adage in Latin, to make it absolutely clear, and I was very grateful for it. I don't know whether Geoff took this advice to heart though. Father Breen explained to us that his attitude towards betting on the races was similar to his job, because in his job he needed faith and hope most of all.

Then I glanced up and inadvertently caught sight of a young couple kissing on a balcony. They were on this walkway between two big buildings, and I looked up through the sunlight, and in the long shadows this young couple were kissing in a romantic, passionate, Romeo-and-Juliet way. It is the only accurate way to describe them. I believe that is an incredibly good portent. It's no good if you sort of wait in bushes with binoculars trying to spot people kissing, but when your eyes *happen* to stumble across what I saw on the Ballymun Estate, I think it's a clear sign that something very good is going to happen.

I thought this might mean that Father Breen's horse, Onewonone, was going to win that afternoon at the Curragh, so I gave Geoff £10 to put on it to win. It didn't win, but I didn't mind. We still managed to have a very pleasant day's racing, in spite of the rain. Dear Father Breen was very sorry about our loss, but there was really no need for him to apologize, because it wasn't his fault at all. It just showed what a nice man he is.

We were very lucky to get a chance to chat with Ronnie Drew. He used to have his own band, called, I think, the Ronnie Drew Band, and then he was in the Dubliners. We went to a pub where they all used to play.

Ronnie sang us a song written by Patrick Kavanagh in which he speaks about himself a hundred years from now. In other words, if Kavanagh came back a hundred years after he died, and wandered round the pubs as a ghost, what would people be saying about him? Or would anybody remember him? And in the song he looks himself up in a book, and the book more or less says that he could have tried harder. It's a really good song, and it illustrates the poetry that can happen in places like these Irish pubs.

A real Irish pub is lovely. However, one of the people we met was a man who sells entire pubs. He sells Irish pub interiors to hotels around the world, and he showed me a list of where he'd sold these pubs. They are now featured in every single country which you could possibly imagine around the world. From Fiji to Florence, from Bangkok to Birmingham, there's always an Irish pub. This particular company supplies everything: the training, the fittings, the pictures for the walls, everything. I didn't tell him this at the time, but I thought the whole concept was really atrocious – the vilest trade that anyone could be involved in. All those breweries ripping the interiors out of pubs,

I think is the most disgusting thing anyone has ever done. In fact I would publicly give an award for the pub interior that has not changed for the longest period of time. Mindless breweries think they'll get more money by turning them into theme pubs and of course they've ripped the whole soul and heart out of the pub and the local community. It's one of the only things that I might bring capital punishment back for.

To cheer myself and my readers up, I'll describe my favourite pub of all time, which, of course, is the Lamb in Northumberland. I'd use that as an example of the perfect pub. It was decorated in 1947: Formica-topped tables, cream, now mottled with smoke; glossy cream walls and ceiling; wooden bar; wooden drawer for the money. Lovely. Two neon strip-lights. I would say that's probably the best pub I've ever been in. Generally, hotel bars and theme pubs are used by people who just don't know any better. If you ask where the very old people drink in a town, you might just find a reasonable pub.

For me that was the great thing about Ireland – the Irish and their pubs have so far managed to retain their soul and not been taken over by this awful new world of 'themes'.

Another man I had in the back of the Rolls with me was David Norris, a member of the Irish parliament. He gave me a shortish literary history of Dublin and described the Book of Kells to us. This is an ancient record, kept in Trinity College, and he said literary history started with this book. He made sure we realized that Dublin was really a very literary place altogether.

He made a very interesting point about how the Irish use language, Dubliners in particular. They have a particular turn of phrase which is now being invaded by standardized English. (Actually he used the term 'BBC English'. I'm not sure what he meant – I don't think people speak like that any more, even on the BBC. Not like the old days, like the man who announced that war had broken out in 1939. These days, it's

David Norris

all Zoe Ball and Jools Holland, that sort of stuff. But, on the plus side,
I suppose a world war isn't breaking out.)

So to end the chapter I think I'll suggest my readers join me by raising
their glasses with a typical toast to the patron saint of Ireland that I was
told by one of the cab drivers in the Café No Name. It goes something
like this: 'St Patrick was a gentleman, who through strategy and stealth
banished all the snakes from Ireland. Here's a toasting to his health (but
not too many toastings lest you lose yourself, forget good St Patrick, and
then see all those snakes back again).'

Budapest

One night when I was about fifteen or sixteen, my friend Simon Ellis and I were walking along the back streets of Greenwich, past the old docks. As we went past this pub we heard this joyful singing, the song which goes, 'Val-de-ree, val-de-ra, val-de-ree', and then everyone joins in with 'A-ha-ha-ha-ha-ha-ha-ha!'. It sounded like synchronized laughing, and we both thought, Hey, this is the pub for us.

It was a jolly family pub in those days, which meant old people in suits and ties, a couple of toughies, a general mix of people. They had a pianist whose name was Adam. He was about sixty with big whiskers, and he drank pints of milk. He was rather Victorian-looking: a smiley face, greased-back hair and sitting on a high piano stool which he brought in himself. (Adam was a pseudonym, chosen because his girlfriend was called Eve, but he wasn't supposed to be with her. Once he looked at me all earnestly and said, 'You know, I've stuck with the one woman for a long time, and I think it's important to do that. But whatever you do, don't tell the wife.')

People would get up and sing from time to time. When it was my turn I got up and played a bit of piano. Adam could tell from my style that I was a bit of a boogie-head. I might have played 'Georgia On My Mind', something like that. He asked me to do a duet. He was a brilliant stride pianist – and I mean brilliant, because he could do Fats Waller with exactly the right feel. I learnt a lot of stride piano from him. He was a natural musician, swung like a donkey's bollocks. He was marvellous. When he said, 'Do you want to do a Fats Waller duet?' that was a bit tricky; I would have a go at it now with him, but when I was sixteen it was a bit much for me, although I wanted to learn. So he said, 'Let's try this song instead,' and shouted out the chords as we went along. It was called 'Bar Me and Mr Shane', and it was similar to an American pop hit but the chords come from a very old Middle European, Jewish folk-song tradition. We would start off very slow, with arpeggios, and then he'd start to shout the chords out and we would get faster and faster until the whole pub was heaving, jumping up and down with excitement. The whole place did a mad Middle European dance for those moments, and then it would go back to somebody singing 'My Old Man's a Dustman'. Magical evenings.

There was another song we used to do called 'Black Eyes', which is an old Russian folk dance. This was my first introduction, I suppose, to Middle European music and the excitement and magic of it. I think it had the same effect on me as listening to rock and roll or ska records. These were London people who were used to shouting, 'Doing the Lambeth walk, oy!', but they immediately cottoned on to the vibe of this. So I feel nostalgic for those evenings in that pub – bare-knuckle fighters preparing themselves in the corner and hussies with their lipstick on. But enough of me.

The population of Hungary is 10.4 million, the population of Budapest 2 million. It used to be a much larger country, 70 per cent bigger than it is now. It is landlocked between east and west Europe, and it's bordered by seven different countries. Budapest is divided into two parts by the River Danube: Buda and Pest. Buda is the old part of town, surrounded by medieval battlements, and very picturesque, although the whole scene is slightly marred by the modern Hilton Hotel, which has been plonked in the middle of it.

On our first evening we ate in a restaurant where a man was playing an instrument like a piano, except that he had to hit the strings with hammers himself instead of having the piano do it for him. It was like a cross between a vibraphone and a piano. It's called the zymbali, I believe, and jolly good it was too. It was like being in *The Third Man*. Vienna is only a few hours from here.

The next morning we set off to look at possible locations, and everybody seemed very friendly and helpful, with the exception of our bus driver, who was the most gloomy and incompetent twerp I have ever come across in my life. He would drive straight into a traffic jam, which was out of our way in the first place, and then park us miles from our destination.

For example, we wanted to look at a particular statue, on the side of a hill overlooking the city. The driver parked at the top of the hill and then refused to move, saying that there was no access to the statue by road. So we had to scramble down the side of the mountain to get to it. Geoff said somebody was bound to break their ankle, and then my agent said, 'Yes I'm very worried because I don't think Jools is insured.' So they weren't worried about me hurting myself – just about the insurance angle. Anyway, we tumbled down the mountain to the statue, only to find a perfectly good main road at its base.

The other statues we saw were all relics of the Communist era. The Soviet government took over running Hungary in 1948 until Communism fell apart in 1989. But in the meantime they had littered the whole of Hungary with these gigantic statues of Lenin, Marx and Engels, and of course Communist soldiers marching, etc. After 1989 the Hungarians

Budapest

took all these sculptures out of their public places, because they didn't want to look at them any more, and put them in a specially built park in an out-of-the-way suburb. The walls are made of red plumbing bricks, which we use in Britain for sewers. Altogether it is like walking into a de Chirico painting, because you see these bright red bricks and these strange,enormous sculptures of the proletariat all crammed together. It gave me a good opportunity to tell my joke: 'Why do Communists only drink herbal teas? Because they believe that property is theft.'

At the gift shop I bought some Communist medals and passes, and CDs of songs of the revolution. I bought lots of those as gifts for friends, because I have friends on all sides of the political fence, and quite a few sitting on top of it.

I did almost feel a twinge of pity for Karl Marx, because there was a picture of him on a T-shirt with a Coca-Cola sign next to his face, representing everything he was against. I think it was a bit cruel really. I mean, I might not have agreed with most of his ideas but I think he's probably right about Coca-Cola. Anyway, he was only doing his best.

I'd read that the huge antiquated amusement park had been unchanged for thirty or forty years. I rather liked the sound of this, bearing in mind that old amusement parks are one of the most dangerous places you can be, especially a one-time Eastern Bloc one, probably made of timber and rusty low-quality metal.

My son George wanted to go on a ride, so he climbed up with Paul, my agent. It looked like it was just going to bump them up in the air in a rather sedate manner. As there were only two of them, the people that ran the machine were reluctant to get it going. After a lot of talking through an interpreter, and bribing and shouting, they started it going. Then, after about a minute I realized that it was one of the most dangerous rides I'd ever seen, twisting upside-down and sideways at great speed. George wasn't strapped in properly and looked as though he was going to fall out. So within a minute of me bribing and shouting at them to get it going I had to do the same again to make them stop it.

Budapest has a very big Jewish population (Tony Curtis was born here). In the Dohany Synagogue (the second biggest in the world), there's a silver tree with silver leaves to represent (I think) the twenty thousand people who were taken and killed by the Nazis at the end of the war. Bob Cohen, an American living in Budapest, explained to me that the Hungarian government had been rather anti-semitic, but they disliked the Germans even more. So they protected people from being taken away by the Nazis until the very end of the war, but then there was nothing they could do because it got out of control.

Bob played some Jewish folk music for us. He played the violin and his friend accompanied him on the guitar. He explained that the gypsies and Jews always had bands together before the war. By the end of the war so many Jews had been killed that it was the gypsies who kept the songs going. Songs like that are remembered by ear, they're not written down.

Later, we filmed a marvellous group called Ando Drom (On the Road). They began as a music theatre group in the eighties, and had all been part of a gypsy children's summer camp run by a Romany cultural institution. Their music is based on the 'wandering gypsy' tradition, which means that their voices often have to make up for a lack of instruments, for which they also tend use everyday objects. Ando Drom have taken some of these traditional songs and added a modern feel to them.

As we were planning to film the brilliant improvisational alto-sax player Mihaly Dresch. I spent some time going through a CD of his music. There was this mournful Transylvanian folk song, whose chords were so sad that I was almost in tears with the beauty and simplicity of them. Dresch's quartet play a cross between traditional Hungarian music and jazz. This track which had caught my ear was a ballad, almost a lament, that reminded me of the blues.

When we were ready to rehearse the song, I went to open the piano and it was locked. (Now that's one of the worst things ever. When I was a child I used to have nightmares about coming across a piano, wanting to play it, and it being locked.) So, I regret to say, I forced the lid: snapping the lock and buckling the wood. People might say that's a good reason for locking a piano, that type of behaviour, but if they didn't lock the piano there would be nothing to be broken. I should point out that we did try to get the key first, it wasn't just a straightforward act of vandalism or impatience. Dresch was rather gentle, a sort of free spirit, and he seemed a little bit surprised at my behaviour, but over the years I've come across this sort of thing quite a few times. As it always does, it made me very angry, and this time I snapped.

Anyway, I asked Dresch to translate the words of the song, and the first verse I rather liked; it went along the lines of 'You're my sweetheart and I went to the river last night and I had a horrible dream that you

Magical evenings with Middle European music

One of only three 1958 Wartburgs in the world?

didn't love me any more and you left me and went off with another.' The next verse is: 'My dream was true, you have gone off with another, and I would just like you, when you're with him, to reflect on the fact that I still love you but I don't blame you or anything, it's all right, I just want you to be happy.' Which again I rather liked. It was like a blues song: nice simple chords and sentiments we could all identify with. However, the last verse slightly lost me: 'When you have a piece of bread, always think of me; I know you're with your boyfriend, but when you have your bread, look at it and remember me.' I would have edited it, myself.

For my transport around Budapest, we were going to get a Wartburg. Having made a few enquiries about the car, I discovered it was to be a 1962 model, but when it arrived and we checked the chassis numbers, it seemed to be a 1958 car. I think that makes it one of only three in the world.

Let me give you a little history of the Wartburg. The company was put together between 1894 and 1902. They made the large, button-seat, veteran type of vehicles that we see in the London-to-Brighton run. The name then went into a sort of obscurity, but eventually they were bought up by BMW in the 1930s. BMW are not clever or inventive on their own; they started off making English Austin 7s under licence, and then made Wartburgs before making BMWs in their own right.

This particular car was made in Eisenach, in East Germany, and its badge is a lovely little picture of the Eisenach Auto Factory. It is about the size of an MGB, has a front-wheel drive so that the floor is completely flat, and an extraordinary three-cylinder 900cc two-stroke engine. It's surprisingly zippy at low speeds, and rather well engineered.

We started off by driving past St Stephen's Basilica, which contains the relics of St Stephen's hand (which was cut off). St Stephen, of course, was the first king of Hungary to convert to Christianity, persuaded by Pope Sylvester. Hungary was mostly pagan at that time, so St Stephen wrote long theses about how it was good to live in harmony and be tolerant in a multi-cultural society. Also I think he used to gouge out the pagans' eyes if they didn't agree with him. St Stephen's is the main church, and it looks like our own St Paul's, the jewel in London's architectural crown.

When we stopped to film outside the Transport Museum, we saw the most incredible thing, a giant pedal car. It was like a Morris Minor or something, full size. If we had things like that in London, think how little pollution there would be. There would still be just as much silliness and argument over parking, but what a treat it would be.

We drove around some more, ending up in Heroes Square. This is a lovely great big Ben-Hur affair. A 118-foot fluted column dominates the scene, with a gigantic Corinthian capital on the top, surmounted by a statue of the Archangel Gabriel. At its base are statues of all the different heroes of Hungary, leaders of the seven tribes (whoever they were) and important-looking people on horses. It was built in 1896 to commemorate the millennium of Magyar rule. On either side there's these Roman- and Greek-style buildings which contain art galleries. One of them houses one of the greatest collections in the world: Old Masters, the lot.

Then I spotted an ice-cream seller whom I thought must be a spy. I could just imagine myself as a 1960s-style spy: the Saint; James Bond; Jools Holland, Our Man in Budapest. You would be sent to meet your connection, who would be the Ice-Cream Man in Heroes Square; he'd give you your mission. And the only other person in this whole square was a man who was acting very suspiciously. It was the hottest day of the year, sweltering, and he had a little stall next to the ice-cream man, selling thick woollen jumpers. Who was going to buy these? Who would even approach him? So I went up to him in a covert sort of way, and said: 'Is it busy today?' He just said, 'Hello!' without giving anything away. So then I tested him further: 'Do we wait for Red October in the springtime?', looking at him meaningfully. He just said, 'Yes.' He had a moustache and I guessed it was false. I was going to try to tear it from him and reveal his true identity, but the crew advised me not to.

There's a lot of people around these parts who look as though they might be spies to me. Take the New York Café. It was built in the late 1890s in the baroque style, with barley-sugar columns, and cherubs, and mirrors, and bull lamps, and it has a great Middle European glamour to it. All I could see in there were spies everywhere I looked.

It was also a meeting place for artists, political thinkers, intellectuals, celebrities, and the like. Sometimes people couldn't pay for their coffee or food, so they would write a poem or an article, or do a drawing, things like that. People like Alexander Korda, the film director, or Pelé, the footballer, they've all been in there – but I think Pelé, probably had enough money for the coffee.

The story of Count Dracula originates in Transylvania, which was once part of Hungary. Bram Stoker got a lot of his inspiration from a Hungarian who was a British government spy – a well-respected man

Unable to compare with the mighty British bikes – but what could?

whose name was Armin Vambery. Vambery travelled around collecting strange stories that people had about blood-sucking, and unpleasant creatures of the night, but they were based largely on two characters who did actually exist.

One was Countess Elizabeth Bathory (1560–1613), who believed that if she bathed in the blood of virgins she would extend her own life indefinitely. She killed some 650 unfortunates, but only lived to be fifty-three, so it was all rather a waste of time. The other one was Vlad the Impaler (whose father was Count Dracula). Vlad was known as a bit of a hard nut and was generally as unpleasant as his name implies. For instance, when three dignitaries came to his castle (possibly to complain about some of his activities), they didn't take their hats off when they were addressing him. He took this to be a sign of enormous disrespect and had their hats nailed to their heads. Legend has it that he went off to fight the Turks, and soon after, word came back to his wife that he had been killed in battle. She was so upset that she went and killed herself – although you would have thought, the type of bloke he was, it would have been a bit of a relief. However, he hadn't been killed after all. When he came home to discover what had happened to Mrs Dracula, he was so furious that he made a pact with the devil to live for ever so he could wreak his fury on humanity. (Bela Lugosi, who played the first Dracula, was in fact the Hungarian Minister of Culture. He left for Hollywood in 1917.)

Anyway we explained all this outside Castle Vajdahunyad in the centre of Budapest; it looked very vampiric and Geoff put his vampire teeth in and chewed blood capsules. In fact Geoff really seemed to be enjoying himself on this particular location. When we got back to the hotel we got into the lift with lots of bigwig people, Chinese, Americans, and so forth, and he slipped the teeth in again to frighten them. Half the people thought it was hilarious and the other half ignored him. I won't bother to say which half I was in. I love Geoff.

My postscript to the whole Dracula thing is that these days people are far more aware than before that you can't mix certain sorts of blood. So apart from the fact that bathing in virgins' blood doesn't work as a life lengthener, it might very well *shorten* your life. My advice is, don't do it.

I really enjoy markets filled with junk, second-hand goods, old books and bits of machinery. They're handy if you're intending to pick up an old Rembrandt, a piece of Meccano, a rusting garden tool or a bootleg CD.

You can usually find one or two redeeming features in any situation, and the Russian occupation of Hungary did leave behind some very interesting militaria. At the Ecseri flea market George bought a disused hand grenade, if there is such a thing, and I bought a Soviet-made compass.

There was a great selection of Eastern-made motor bikes, some of which I had never even seen before. There was the Zündapp, which is East German, a contemporary of BMW, and very powerful-looking. There was a Hungarian-made Panini motor bike which had been perfectly restored. I was quite impressed, because although I am a motor-head I had never heard of any of these bikes. Obviously there wasn't anything to compare with the mighty Vincents or Nortons or Triumphs that Britain made, but then what could?

Zoltan Kocsis is the leader of the National Philharmonic Orchestra, and one of the world's greatest concert pianists. He is also the best living interpreter of the Hungarian composer Béla Bartók. Bartók wrote a series entitled 'Ten Easy Piano Pieces': like anything good, they sound easy, but playing them well is very difficult. He collected hundreds of folk tunes and incorporated them into his compositions, believing (as many other great composers do) that the simplicity, beauty and integrity of old folk melodies are as great as anything a top composer could think up for himself. Furthermore, he believed that anybody who hasn't listened to, or been influenced by, folk music and its simplicity has completely missed out.

Our man in Budapest

Zoltan had to be filmed in one particular concert hall, the Vigado, because he said it contained the only piano that was suitable for him. He seemed to be a little bit tetchy at first – but I rather liked this about him, and I think in fact that the man's a genius.

We set up some dry-ice machines to diffuse the light. As all the dry-ice smoke started pouring in, Zoltan said, 'I don't know if I can perform in all this.' Geoff retorted rather gruffly, 'Well, you're not singing, are you?' Zoltan went off looking a bit annoyed, and Geoff asked me, 'Do we really need this man?, I explained to Geoff that he was one of the greatest concert pianists in the world and, furthermore, he was Hungarian, and was going to be playing pieces by one of the greatest Hungarian composers of all time, Béla Bartók, and we also happened to be in

One of the Italian pan pipe players with half a garden fence

Hungary making this film. So yes, I thought, we *did* need him. And could Geoff keep his views to himself.

Then, because of the way the light was shining on the piano, the shadows being cast by the black keys were quite long. Zoltan said he didn't know if he could operate with all of this going on, that the shadows on the piano keys were far too long for him. Now I had never heard this complaint before, and was so impressed by it for sheer pickiness that I thought: I shall use that one myself the first chance I get. Of course, he was right to get everything to his satisfaction before starting to play. But his attitude was in strong contrast to Ruben González who, you will recall, when presented with a dreadful piano in Havana, said: 'This piano is shit . . . but I've played much worse.'

Zoltan played an enchanting piece with absolute brilliance. Some musicians are what I would describe as 'natural'. In other words they've learnt by ear, as most pop musicians do. Other people learn to read music, and they can never get away from that, so although technically they are very good, they don't always have a 'feel'. Ideally, what you want is good technique but not to let that spoil your feel; and to have good feel, but enough technique not to limit this. Zoltan had a brilliant technique but also a completely natural feel for the piano, and I think that's why he is such a genius.

I loved talking to him too; he told me about the people who had played in the Vigado Hall – everybody: Rachmaninov, Debussy, and of course the greatest romantic Hungarian pianist, Franz Liszt. Hungary has a huge musical tradition. People play everywhere – in restaurants, in bars, on the street – and the quality of the musicianship is very good. I said this to Zoltan, and he said that he found it really annoying when violinists came up to him in a restaurant and played in his face. I said, 'Yes but I might point out that in London, where there used to be pianists in every pub, there are now none.' London is a city of 10 million people, but there are fewer musicians than I saw in Budapest, a city of 2 million. I think he could see the point I was making, and he said, 'You're right, people are playing instruments less and less. Therefore, the audience that come aren't as educated musically as they once were.'

Although the Communists did a lot of awful things, one of the good things they did was to educate people very well. When they were in power, more people were playing instruments, and people would study music in a more serious way. The Communists also supported and paid for orchestras and musicians.

Buda, the old town, is very picturesque, and it differs quite radically from the Pest side of the river. Buda looks Germanic, or Austrian, and has a 'Pinocchio' feel about it. Some of the buildings appeared to be wall-papered on the outside. This is an old technique, painting patterns on the outside of the buildings, and they really were rather pretty.

We were outside the cathedral long enough to see all sorts of goings-on, weddings and so forth. When the horse-drawn carriages came past with the bride and groom in them, old ladies would come out of the cathedral and burst into tears of joy. They tugged at my arm, wanting me to join in, and tears poured down their faces.

Then a huge, moustachioed Italian came up to us, holding a set of Pan pipes, maybe six inches deep and ten inches across. He asked if we wanted to film him. We thought he was probably just some boring drunk, but I thought, 'Let's give him a chance.' Within seconds there were maybe twelve of these Italian men, and they all had Pan pipes ranging from a tiny set, like a little harmonica, to a gigantic set which was, I think, as big as the man holding it. They played this piece which sounded like a merry-go-round that was spinning out of control at a hundred miles an hour. It was the most charming thing any of us had ever seen or heard. We asked them to play it again, so they all gathered around the conductor (who was completely mad and looked like a Walt Disney cartoon) and did it again.

I don't even know what the instruments they were playing were called. I would have asked them, but none of us spoke the same language. We don't know their names or anything, but we knew they were having a very nice time – and so were we.

The key to a lot of the music in Hungary it is that it is not so much written down as passed down by ear. This is very important, because then it is played unchanged for years and years. Jazz, for example, has evolved a great deal, and moved away from its roots. So if you go to a jazz concert now it doesn't sound at all like Louis Armstrong playing in New Orleans

The men of the Serbian Orthodox choir

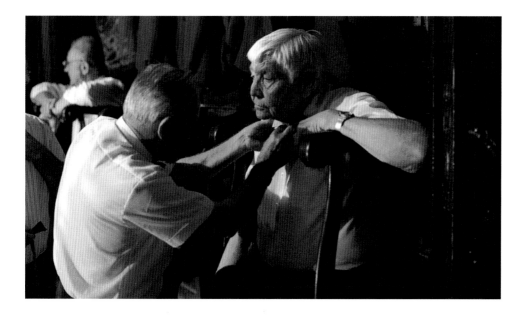

where jazz was actually invented, around the time of the First World War. We went to a club called the Gyoker Dance House to film Piko and his Band, a traditional Hungarian string band, and I could instinctively tell that the sort of people who would have been having a dance in pubs in England in the 1850s would have been dancing to *exactly* this sort of music. It was still exciting to dance to – it hadn't aged at all and had a really robust feel to it. If it had been played the wrong way you wouldn't have wanted to dance, which is the same with any style of music. It doesn't matter how old the piece is, so long as it has got the spirit to it, and gets your own spirit going. Just like Daniel Barenboim said back in Chicago.

For another type of Hungarian music, we went to a Serbian Orthodox church, built in the seventeenth century: it was very pretty and incredibly ornate on the inside. We got a tape of their choir, and they really were extraordinary. It was beautiful, and again it reflected the way music has been passed down unchanged. If you listen to a modern choir in a church in England, it's perfectly good but it doesn't sound as it would

have sounded a hundred years ago. I'm not saying it's right or wrong, it's just the sound of today.

When I heard this Serb choir in person, I was really knocked out. They were all men, over fifty years old – some of them were over sixty, and I wouldn't have been surprised if one or two of them were over eighty. As they sang, I noticed that one of the Hungarian girls who had been helping us with research was crying. I asked her why and she said: 'After they've gone there won't be anybody else left to sing like them, because there are no young ones in the choir, no young people want to join these sorts of choirs.' They had the sound of a lost world.

If I was to take something back as a souvenir from Budapest, it would be the Hello Striptease Club, where Geoff and I popped in for a light ale one evening. Their brochure told us:

Good advice to foreigners. Be determined and do not let apparently helpful taxi drivers or others take you or send you to other places by telling you various misleading explanations, as it is only done by them for the big commission received which will be paid by you in some way.

It was just such an 'apparently helpful taxi driver' who took us to the Hello Club.

Some of the Hungarian people we met had a terrific sense of humour, but I did notice that they have very long memories. One evening, I had just bought the crew a round of drinks. I had a beer and Edit, who was helping us make the film, had a cocktail of some sort. I was saying, 'Cheers!' to people, and I went to clink her glass and she suddenly looked at me very sternly and in a deep Hungarian voice said, 'We must never *ever* toast with beer and put our glasses together. It is considered a very bad sign here, after what happened.' I said, 'Oh, I'm so sorry, what happened?' She explained that there had been a certain massacre by

A quiet moment with Geoff

Austrian soldiers, who then toasted this grisly event with beer glasses. I said, 'Oh, that's awful, I'm sorry. When did this happen?' She then told me it was 1831 or something. That's quite a long time ago, isn't it?

Afterword

Some people just like travelling. I don't. Once I've gone I enjoy it, but the idea of setting off and travelling just exhausts me.

One of the *good* things about travelling is learning more about airports and how they work. I never used to be interested in planes but I am a bit now, especially as I'm in them so much. I came back from Japan the other day, and had the treat of going in the cockpit. You need to know someone, or be invited to visit the captain. I'm not sure what other ways there are to get up there; I don't think pretending to hijack the plane is a very good idea.

Of course, travel does broaden the mind. I always have a very open mind about wherever I'm going. In fact, before each programme I had no idea of what I was going to do. We've gone in and treated each place as a blank canvas, reacting to the place in a spontaneous way.

It's exciting flying over a foreign landscape or city, and coming in to land there; but it's always a much greater thrill for me flying over Belmarsh Prison at City Airport. That's always the bit I look forward to most. The great thing about travelling is the coming home, if you ask me. As Mr Pooter says in *The Diary of a Nobody*, 'What's the good of a home, if you're never in it?'

Going home

I was very pleased to leave a headstone for one of the most important blues pianists in the world. For me, that made the whole trip to Chicago worthwhile.